Pirates Through the Ages

Cumulative Index

Pirates Through the Ages

Cumulative Index

Jennifer Stock, Index Coordinator

GALE
CENGAGE Learning

Detroit • New York • San Francisco • New Haven, Conn • Waterville, Maine • London

**Pirates Through the Ages:
Cumulative Index**

Index Coordinator: Jennifer Stock

Rights Acquisition and Management: Robyn
Young

Composition: Evi Abou-El-Seoud

Manufacturing: Wendy Blurton

Imaging: John Watkins

Product Design: Kristine Julien

For product information and technology assistance, contact us at
Gale Customer Support, 1-800-877-4253.
For permission to use material from this text or product,
submit all requests online at **www.cengage.com/permissions.**
Further permissions questions can be emailed to
permissionrequest@cengage.com

Cover photographs reproduced by permission of Mass Communications
Specialist 1st Class Cassandra Thompson/U.S. Navy via Getty Images (U.S.
Navy investigates a suspected Somali pirate skiff), Private Collection/Peter
Newark Historical Pictures/The Bridgeman Art Library International (William
Kidd), and The Art Archive/Granger Collection/The Picture Desk, Inc. (two
pirates fighting, illustration from "Howard Pyle's Book of Pirates," 1921).

While every effort has been made to ensure the reliability of the information
presented in this publication, Gale, a part of Cengage Learning, does not
guarantee the accuracy of the data contained herein. Gale accepts no payment
for listing; and inclusion in the publication of any organization, agency,
institution, publication, service, or individual does not imply endorsement of the
editors or publisher. Errors brought to the attention of the publisher and verified
to the satisfaction of the publisher will be corrected in future editions.

Library of Congress Cataloging-in-Publication Data

Stock, Jennifer York, 1974–
    Pirates through the ages reference library : cumulative index / Jennifer
Stock, index coordinator.
        p. cm.
    Includes index.
    ISBN ISBN 978-1-4144-8666-6
        1. Pirates--History--Indexes. I. Title.

G535.S822 2011
    910.4'5--dc22

2010051979

Gale
27500 Drake Rd.
Farmington Hills, MI, 48331-3535

ISBN-13: 978-1-4144-8662-8 (set)
ISBN-13: 978-1-4144-8663-5
(Almanac)
ISBN-13: 978-1-4144-8664-2
(Biographies)
ISBN-13: 978-1-4144-8665-9
(Primary Sources)
ISBN-13: 978-1-4144-8666-6
(Cumulative Index)

ISBN-10: 1-4144-8662-6 (set)
ISBN-10: 1-4144-8663-4
(Almanac)
ISBN-10: 1-4144-8664-2
(Biographies)
ISBN-10: 1-4144-8665-0
(Primary Sources)
ISBN-10: 1-4144-8666-9
(Cumulative Index)

This title is also available as an e-book.
ISBN-13: 978-1-4144-8667-3 ISBN-10: 1-4144-8667-7
Contact your Gale, a part of Cengage Learning sales representative for
ordering information.

Printed in Singapore
1 2 3 4 5 6 7 15 14 13 12 11

Index

Bold type indicates major entries. Illustrations are marked by (ill.).

A: Pirates Through the Ages: Almanac, B: Pirates Through the Ages: Biographies, PS: Pirates Through the Ages: Primary Sources.

A

A Cruising Voyage Round the World (Rogers)
  B: 214
A General History of the Robberies and Murders of the Most Notorious Pirates (Johnson)
  A: 97–98, 103, 108–9, 118, 130–31, 133–34, 222, 223 (ill.), 224–25, 227, 228
  B: 29, 51–52, 218
  PS: 73, 77, 83, 87, 88
A New Voyage Round the World (Dampier)
  B: 68
Abuse of sailors by captains
  A: 119, 128
Accomplices and accessories to piracy crimes
  PS: 62, 92, 158, 171–72, 180, 181
Aceh, Sumatra, Indonesia
  A: 186 (ill.), 202
Achilles (ship)
  A: 149
Act for the More Effectual Suppression of Piracy (England, 1700s)
  PS: 61–62

Acts of reprisal
  A: 62
  English warfare, A: 29–31, 30 (ill.)
  Greek warfare, A: 8–9
  Scottish pirate usage, A: 31–32
Adams, John
  PS: 44–45, 46, 102
Adams, Robert (captain)
  PS: 37, 42–43
Adams, Robert (pirate kidnapping victim)
  biography, PS: 39, 42
  "Letter from Robert Adams to Captain Robert Adams,"
  PS: 37, 41–43
Admirals
  Kanhoji Angria, B: 1–2
  Barbarossa, B: 11, 15, 73
  Ching-Chi-Ling, B: 142
  Andrea Doria, B: 16, 73–76
  Dragut Reis, B: 71
  John Hawkins, B: 105
  Kwo Lang, B: 58
  Murat Reis, B: 177
  Christopher Myngs, B: 184
  Tz'eun Mao Szun, B: 58
Admiralty courts
  A: 62, 142, 145
  B: 125, 186

Adriatic Sea
  B: 74, 76, 77
Adriatic Sea piracy
  Illyrians, A: 10–11
  Narentines, A: 21
  Uskoks, A: 45
Adventure Galley (ship)
  B: 136–38
Adventure (ship)
  B: 32, 33, 34–36
Adventure stories
  A: 224, 227–29
Aegean Sea
  B: 12–14, 71, 77
Aetolian League
  A: 10
Africa
  Benin, B: 206–7
  Egypt, B: 73
  Somalia and Somali pirates, B: 2–3
  Tripoli, B: 71, 76
  See also Barbary Coast; Tunis; West Africa
African piracy, 21st century. *See* Gulf of Aden; Somali piracy
African slave trade
  PS: 26, 28–32, 45, 73
  See also Slave trade

1

African/African American pirates,
   in crews
   A: 70, 114, 117, 131–32
Agriculture
   Barbary coast, **A:** 38
   Caribbean, **A:** 79; **PS:** 51, 55
   China, **PS:** 113
   Cilicia, **PS:** 20, 21
   Mediterranean coastal
      regions, **A:** 2
   North Africa, **PS:** 39
   Rome, **PS:** 13–14
   Scandinavia, **A:** 22
Air patrols
   A: 201, 202 (ill.), 207
   PS: 175
al-Jalahimah clan
   B: 116
al-Khalifa clan
   B: 115–17, 120–22
al-Shabab (Islamist group)
   A: 212
Alamgir I. *See* Aurangzeb
   (Mughal emperor)
Alaska
   B: 84
Albion (warship)
   B: 51
Alcoholism
   A: 122
Alexander the Great
   A: 10
   PS: 21–22
Algeria
   Algerian pirates, **PS:** 39
   on IP piracy watch list,
      PS: 213
Algiers, Algeria
   A: 35, 36 (ill.), 39, 52, 54,
      55, 55 (ill.)
   B: 14, 75, 176, 177, 178
   PS: 37, 39, 41 (ill.), 42,
      44, 46
Ali, Uluj
   A: 44

Allen, Mel
   excerpt from "Captain
      Richard Phillips and the
      Pirates: What's Ahead for
      the Vermont Captain,"
      PS: 195–98
Alonso, Don
   B: 170
Altium (Australian company)
   PS: 204
Alvilda (Swedish female pirate)
   PS: 70, 71 (ill.)
America (ship)
   A: 151
American Civil War (1861–65)
   A: 154–55
American colonies
   anti-pirate activity, **PS:** 62
   Continental Congresses,
      A: 137–38
   French support, **A:** 146–47
   governors, **A:** 103, 105, 114
   history, **A:** 141
   independence, **A:** 54
   pirate activity, **PS:** 44, 61
   privateering interest, **A:** 103,
      105, 137, 139
   privateering use and
      regulation, **A:** 139–45, 144
      (ill.), 146–47, 149–55
   trade laws, **A:** 100, 137, 139
   See also American Revolution
      (1775–83); American
      Revolution (1775–83);
      United States
American Revolution (1775–83)
   B: 123, 126, 131
   PS: 44, 97, 98 (ill.), 102,
      105, 158
   beginning, **A:** 137–39
   British privateering, **A:** 145
   naval forces and strategy,
      A: 139–40, 147–49
   privateer use/success, **A:** 141,
      142–45, 146–47, 149–55

American sovereignty
   A: 146
Americas
   as slave trade destination,
      PS: 26, 28–32, 45
   North American coast, **B:** 26,
      29, 38–39, 84
   South America, **B:** 79, 184
   Spanish trade colonies,
      B: 184
   See also Caribbean Sea and
      islands; North America,
      east coast pirate activity;
      South America; Spanish
      Main; United States
Amnesty. *See* Pardons and
   amnesty
Amputation
   PS: 130, 141
Anatolia
   Ottoman Turks' control,
      A: 38
   recordkeeping, **A:** 4
   Roman conquest, **A:** 10
Ancient Egypt
   art and architecture, **A:** 4,
      5 (ill.)
   ports, **A:** 3
   recordkeeping, **A:** 4
Ancient Greece
   civilization, **A:** 4, 6; **PS:** 2, 4,
      5, 9
   historical perspectives, **A:** 6–8
   language, **A:** 7
   literature, **A:** 6–8
   pirate concepts, **A:** 6, 7
   records, **PS:** 2, 3
   Trojan War and aftermath,
      PS: 2–3, 5–7
   warfare and piracy, **A:** 8–10
Ancient Rome
   piracy, **A:** 10–15, 11 (ill.), 36
   pirate concepts, **A:** 7, 198–99
   sea raiders, **A:** 1
   wars, **A:** 11

Ancient world, and piracy
  A: 1–15, 3 (ill.), 5 (ill.), 11
    (ill.), 36
Anglo-Dutch Treaty (1824)
  A: 174
  PS: 170
Anglo-Dutch War, First
  (1652–54)
  B: 184
Anglo-Dutch War, Second
  (1665–67)
  B: 189
Anglo-Spanish War (1655–60)
  B: 166, 188
Angre, Kanhoji. *See* Angria,
  Kanhoji
Angria, Conajee. *See* Angria,
  Kanhoji
Angria, Kanhoji
  A: 171–73
  B: 1–9
  alliances with European
    pirates, **B:** 9
  capturing European ships,
    strategies, **B:** 1–9
  career success, **B:** 4–6, 8–9
  defeat of Tolaji Angria, **B:** 8
    (ill.), 9
  early life, **B:** 1–2
  peace treaty with England,
    B: 6
Angria, Tolaji
  B: 8 (ill.), 9
Anti-Counterfeiting Trade
  Agreement (ACTA)
  PS: 213
Anti-Piracy Caucus.
  See Congressional International
  Anti-Piracy Caucus
Anti-privateering laws
  B: 223
Antigua
  B: 135
Antigua (ship)
  B: 135

Antipiracy campaigns
  PS: 157
  Africa/Gulf of Aden region,
    A: 193, 204–7, 206 (ill.),
    210–11, 211 (ill.), 212–14
  Ancient Greece, **A:** 9; **PS:** 9
  Ancient Rome, **A:** 11, 11
    (ill.), 14–15
  Bahamas, **B:** 211, 214–16
  against Barbary corsairs,
    A: 35, 54–55
  British Piracy Act (1721),
    B: 206
  China, **A:** 167, 169, 180–81;
    B: 58, 142; **PS:** 111–12,
    113–14
  cross-country teamwork,
    A: 197, 201, 202 (ill.), 205,
    206–7, 209
  end to privateering, **PS:** 102,
    103
  England and Great Britain,
    A: 28–29, 31, 33, 54, 55,
    55 (ill.), 109–10, 110–11,
    113–15, 115 (ill.), 174,
    175
  English in Caribbean, **B:** 63,
    172, 188–89, 206–9
  English in India, **B:** 6–8, 102
  English in Mediterranean,
    B: 222–24
  France, **A:** 54, 55, 203–4
  global, 18th century, **A:** 177
  Hanseatic League, **A:** 26–27,
    28
  Holy League, **B:** 73–74
  Jamaica, **B:** 173
  Manchus, **B:** 144
  naval efforts and forces,
    A: 206–7, 206 (ill.), 209,
    210, 213
  Netherlands, **A:** 174; **B:** 177
  Portugal, **B:** 6–7
  Richard Coote, **B:** 136–38
  Roman empire, **PS:** 9, 19–21

  ships' captains, **PS:** 62,
    64–65, 66, 85
  Somali piracy, **PS:** 185,
    186–87
  Southeast Asia and Strait of
    Malacca, **A:** 185–87, 187
    (ill.), 201–3, 202 (ill.)
  Spain, **B:** 159
  Strait of Malacca, **PS:** 169,
    170, 174–76, 174–77
  21st century, **A:** 185–87, 187
    (ill.), 197–214, 202 (ill.),
    206 (ill.), 211 (ill.)
  United States, **A:** 54–55, 154,
    206–7, 206 (ill.), 209
  wasted political opportunities,
    A: 25, 54, 197
Antipiracy laws
  Ancient Rome, **A:** 13, 14, 15
  England, and end to piracy's
    golden age, **PS:** 61–62, 92,
    158
  Great Britain, **A:** 114, 134
  international, and agencies,
    modern era, **A:** 180,
    200, 201, 204–6, 208–9,
    210
  international law, **PS:** 103–4,
    157–58, 167, 186, 199
  IP piracy and copyright,
    PS: 203, 204, 208, 210,
    211, 213
  United Nations Conference
    on the Law of the Sea
    (UNCLOS), **PS:** 157–67
  See also Antipiracy campaigns;
    Maritime law
Antony, Marc
  A: 14
Aphrodite (goddess)
  PS: 2
Apple
  A: 185
Arab Navy Task Force
  A: 207, 209

Arabian Sea
   B: 2–4, 9
Argentina, on IP piracy watch list
   PS: 213
Ariffin, John
   PS: 172–74
Armada, Spanish
   B: 85–86, 112
Artifacts
   B: 25, 25 (ill.), 33, 84
Artillery
   B: 24
Artists
   intellectual property ownership
     rights, **PS:** 203, 205, 207
   painters, **PS:** 126, 127
Artists' illustrations of pirates
   A: 229, 230 (ill.)
Aruj Barbarossa
   A: 39–41, 40 (ill.)
   B: 11–14
Arviragus and Philicia (play)
   A: 220
Asia. *See* China; Formosa; India;
   Indonesia; Japan; Korea; Malay
   Peninsula/Malaysia piracy;
   Singapore; Strait of Malacca;
   Vietnam
Asian financial crisis
   A: 183
Assassination, Roman politics
   PS: 15, 21
Assimilation, Vikings
   A: 22, 24, 25
Asylum
   A: 210
Athena (goddess)
   PS: 2, 7
Athens (city-state)
   A: 8, 9
Atlantic Ocean
   B: 18, 22, 37, 201
Attacks
   deceit in initiating, **A:** 47, 89,
     103–4, 126, 130

incidents in 2010, **A:** 186
   (ill.), 198 (ill.), 212–13
methods and weapons,
   A: 47–48, 127–28, 166,
   168, 172, 177, 183–85,
   188, 190
planning, **A:** 172, 184;
   PS: 171, 171 (ill.), 181,
   184, 194
Auctions, slaves
   PS: 40, 41 (ill.)
Augustine, St.
   A: 10
Aurangzeb (Mughal emperor)
   B: 97
Australia
   B: 3, 68
Austria
   A: 45
Authorship debates
   A: 222
   PS: 87–88
Automatic weapons
   A: 177, 183, 190, 193 (ill.)
Avatar (film, 2009)
   PS: 205
Avery, Henry. *See* Every, Henry
Aztecs
   A: 59, 60

B

Bachelor's Delight (ship)
   B: 66–67
Baghlahs (ships)
   B: 118
Bahadur, Jay
   excerpt from "I'm Not a
     Pirate, I'm the Saviour of
     the Sea," **PS:** 183–86
Bahamas
   governors, **B:** 211, 215–18
   pirate havens, **B:** 22, 30, 39,
     46, 103, 126, 215

See also Nassau, Bahamas;
   New Providence, Bahamas
Bahamas piracy
   A: 106–7, 108, 109–10,
     110–11, 112
   PS: 62, 63
Bahrain
   B: 115–17, 120–21
Bainbridge (warship)
   PS: 194, 196–97, 198,
     200 (ill.)
Bainbridge, William
   PS: 199, 200 (ill.)
Baldridge, Adam
   A: 100
Balinini people
   A: 174
Baltic Sea
   antipiracy campaigns, **A:** 26
   trade, **A:** 25, 26
   Victual Brothers piracy,
     A: 26–28
   Viking piracy, **A:** 17, 24
Baltimore, Ireland
   B: 175, 178–80
Ban Ki-moon
   A: 213
Banishment
   PS: 57, 114
Barataria, Louisiana
   B: 151–54, 156
Barbados
   A: 78, 79, 128
   B: 30–31, 37–39, 40 (ill.),
     166, 205
Barbarian Cruelty (Brooks)
   PS: 40
Barbarossa
   A: 39–41
   B: 11–19, 11 (ill.)
   Aruj (brother), piracy
     partnership, **A:** 39–40;
     B: 11–14
   career, **A:** 40–41; **B:** 14–18
   Dragut Reis and, **B:** 73–74

early life, **B:** 12

tomb, **B:** 17 (ill.)

Barbary Coast

    A: 35, 36 (ill.), 38, 55

    B: 11, 13–14, 71, 175–78

Barbary corsairs

    A: 35, 38–41, 43–55, 57, 177

    PS: 37–46, 38 (ill.), 41 (ill.),
       117

    Barbarossa, **B:** 11–18

    Barbarossa Brothers,
       A: 39–41, 40 (ill.)

    battles with Knights of Malta,
       B: 180

    Byzantine Empire defenses,
       A: 19

    decline and legacy, **A:** 54–55,
       197

    Dragut Reis, **B:** 71, 73

    galley slaves, **B:** 15

    Knights of Malta and,
       A: 41–44

    literary portrayals, **A:** 231, 232

    Murat Reis, **B:** 176–78

    piracy phases, **A:** 35

    renegades, **A:** 51–54

    ships, **A:** 35, 39, 45–47, 46
       (ill.), 53

    slave trade, **A:** 41, 47, 48–50,
       49 (ill.), 51, 53, 54

    John Ward, **B:** 219–20

The Barbary Pirates (Forester)

    A: 224

Barbary Wars

    A: 54–55, 55 (ill.)

    PS: 44, 45, 45 (ill.), 46

Barnet, Jonathan

    B: 51

    PS: 64–65

Barrie, J.M.

    A: 229–31

    B: 218

    PS: 147 (ill.)

    biography, **PS:** 143–44,
       146–48, 154

excerpt from *Peter Pan, or The
    Boy Who Would Not Grow
    Up,* **PS:** 150–52

Peter Pan's Treasure Island
    references, **PS:** 141, 143

**Bartholomew Roberts's Ship's
Articles**

    PS: 73–82

    excerpt from "The Life of
       Captain Roberts"
       (Johnson), **PS:** 78–80

Becher, John Thomas,
    PS: 119

Barton, Andrew
    A: 32–33, 32 (ill.)

Bases. *See* Pirate bases

Bath, North Carolina
    B: 32–34, 41

Battles

    Battle of Concord (1775),
       A: 139, 142

    Battle of Kinsale (1601),
       B: 199

    Battle of Lepanto (1571),
       A: 44, 51

    Battle of Lexington (1775),
       A: 139, 142

    Battle of Mogadishu (1993),
       A: 214

    Battle of New Orleans
       (1815), **A:** 151–52;
       B: 153–54

    Battle of Preveza (1538),
       A: 41; **B:** 74

    Battle of Sandwich (1217),
       B: 92–93, 93 (ill.)

    Bonhomme Richard vs.
       HMS *Serapis* (1779),
       B: 129–31

    England and Spanish Armada
       (1588), **B:** 85–86

    Four Days Battle (1666),
       B: 189, 189 (ill.)

    HMS *Swallow vs. Royal Fortune*
       (1722), **B:** 207–8, 208 (ill.)

San Juan de Ulúa (1567),
    B: 110, 110 (ill.)

Siege of Malta (1565), **B:** 77

Bay of Biscay
    A: 31

Beaufort Inlet, North Carolina
    B: 32–33, 41

Beer, Captain
    A: 108

Beheading
    A: 26, 27, 53, 166

    B: 18, 36, 57, 66, 84, 93
       (ill.), 167

    PS: 109, 110

Beijing, China
    B: 143

Belgium
    Middle Ages military
       conflicts, **A:** 25

    Scottish privateer piracy,
       A: 32

    Viking piracy, **A:** 24

Bellamy, Samuel
    A: 107–8, 117, 132

    B: 21–27

    captain, **B:** 23

    capture of *Whydah,* **B:** 24

    early life and Hornigold
       friendship, **B:** 21–22

Benedictine monks
    B: 89, 94

Benin
    B: 206–7, 208

Bergen, Norway
    A: 28

Berlioz, Hector
    A: 226

Bermuda
    A: 100

Berserkers
    A: 21

Betsy (ship)
    B: 125

Bialuschewski, Arne
    PS: 88

Bible
PS: 76
Bingham, Richard
B: 196, 198
Biographical accounts of pirates
A: 82, 87–88, 97–98, 108–9,
118, 222–25, 223 (ill.), 227
Biographical works of pirates
PS: 73, 77, 83, 84, 88, 117
Bittlestone, Robert
PS: 11
"Black Bart." See Roberts,
Bartholomew
Black Death
A: 28
Black Flag fleet
A: 166
B: 59
The Black Monk. See Eustace the
Monk
The Black Pirate (film, 1926)
A: 232–33
Black pirates
A: 70, 114, 117, 131–32
Black Prince (ship)
A: 147
"Black Sam." See Bellamy,
Samuel
Blackbeard
A: 105, 108–9, 110, 111, 112
(ill.)
B: **29–36**, 29 (ill.), 40 (ill.)
PS: 141, 144
appearance and dress,
A: 108–9, 109 (ill.), 130
Stede Bonnet and, B: 39–41,
40 (ill.)
chronicling, A: 111, 129,
217, 222, 224
crew member for Benjamin
Hornigold, B: 22
film portrayals, A: 233
influence on Anne Bonny,
B: 46
Jolly Roger, B: 49

Jolly Roger flag, A: 126 (ill.)
Robert Maynard duel, B: 35
(ill.), 36
ships, A: 108, 123
threat against Woodes
Rogers, B: 215
threat to burn Boston, B: 27
Blackbeard the Pirate (film, 1952)
A: 233
Blake, Peter
A: 181, 182 (ill.)
Blessed William (ship)
B: 135, 138
Blockades
B: 31–32, 40, 55, 121, 143
Blodget, Henry
PS: 212–13
Bloody Jack (Meyer)
A: 224
Boat people (Vietnam)
A: 177–79, 179 (ill.)
Bogart, Humphrey
B: 179, 179 (ill.)
Bombay, India
B: 1, 4, 5 (ill.), 6–7
Bombay (ship)
B: 6
Bon Homme Richard (navy ship)
A: 148–49, 148 (ill.)
Bonhomme Richard (ship)
B: 129–31, 130 (ill.)
Bonnet, Stede
B: **37–44**, 37 (ill.)
Blackbeard, and, B: 30–33,
39–41
early life, B: 37–38
execution, B: 44
trial, B: 42–43
Bonnet, Thomas
B: 38
Bonny, Anne
A: 133–34, 133 (ill.), 222
B: **45–52**, 45 (ill.)
PS: 61, 62–63, 63 (ill.),
64–70, 72

career, B: 48–50
early life, B: 46
fame, B: 51–52
family, B: 46–47
relationship with Mary Read,
B: 48–49
Bonny, James
B: 46
PS: 63
Books, pirated
PS: 209, 212
Bootlegs. See Intellectual property
piracy
Booty
PS: 3, 75
charitable dividing, A: 27–28,
189–90
dividing methods, PS: 56–57,
80, 96, 105, 109, 185
dividing, pirates, A: 48, 82, 85,
86, 90, 121, 123, 168, 192
dividing, privateers, A: 8, 9, 28,
29–30, 62, 101, 102, 142
division, B: 23, 48, 57, 69,
86, 187
government bribes and
payouts, A: 13–14, 29, 48,
105, 114
government payments,
PS: 28, 34, 35, 59, 85, 96,
103, 107
investors' takes, PS: 28, 96,
105, 181, 185
modern piracy, A: 180, 181,
212, 213; PS: 172, 184, 185
naval obligations, A: 90
pieces of eight, A: 69, 69 (ill.)
port cities' piracy economies,
A: 9, 29, 33, 38, 39, 90, 192
sales, B: 159
secondary theft, PS: 75
seizing from ships, A: 47, 48,
73–74, 101, 102, 103–4,
129, 219
slaves as, B: 107

Spanish theft from Americas,
A: 57, 59–60, 64–65, 68,
70–71
values, **B:** 32, 85, 97–98, 101,
161, 204
wealthy citizens' takes, **PS:** 85
See also Plundering; Treasure
Border patrols
A: 180
Boston, Massachusetts
A: 143, 145
Bourke, Richard "Iron Dick"
B: 194–95
Bourke, Tibbot-ne-Long
B: 196, 199
Bowie, James
B: 155
Boyah (Somali pirate)
PS: 179, 181–86, 187–88
Brasiliano, Roche
A: 87
Brazil
B: 83, 106, 203
modern piracy, **A:** 181, 182
(ill.)
on IP piracy watch list,
PS: 205
Portugal domain, **A:** 59
Bartholomew Roberts piracy,
A: 113
Brethren of the Coast.
See Buccaneers
Bribes
Barbarossa, **B:** 16, 18
Caribbean governors, **B:** 184
Chinese villagers, **B:** 57
William Dampier, **B:** 65
Henry Every, **B:** 103
for safe harbors, **B:** 104
John Ward, **B:** 222–24
See also Accomplices and
accessories to piracy crimes;
Protection payments
Brigantines
A: 125, 139, 145

British Isles, Viking piracy
A: 19–21, 20 (ill.), 24, 25
British Piracy Act (1721)
B: 206
Brooks, Francis
PS: 40
Brutality
B: 65, 101, 117, 125, 190
Bubonic plague
A: 28
Buccaneers
A: 81 (ill.)
B: 64 (ill.)
William Dampier, **B:** 63–68
defined, **A:** 77
described, **B:** 158–59**PS:** 49,
50 (ill.), 51, 54, 55, 56, 57
early, **A:** 79–82
first-hand accounts, **PS:** 52–60,
54 (ill.)
hunting, **B:** 63, 158, 166
Jolly Roger flag, **A:** 126
François L'Olonnais,
B: 158–63
military uses, **B:** 159, 187
Henry Morgan, **B:** 166–73
Christopher Myngs, **B:** 185
pirating activity, **A:** 82–90,
91–95
privateering, **A:** 77
ships, **A:** 82, 83
The Buccaneers of America
(Exquemelin)
A: 82, 86, 87–88
PS: 49–60
excerpt from *The Buccaneers
of America* (Exquemelin),
PS: 54 (ill.), 55–57, 58 (ill.)
Buried treasure
B: 133, 138, 139 (ill.)
PS: 129, 131, 133, 139–40
William Kidd, **A:** 105
Treasure Island, **A:** 227
Burleigh, Joseph
PS: 72

Bushehr, Persia
B: 119–21
Byron. *See* Gordon, George, Lord
Byron
Byronic hero
A: 225, 227
PS: 120, 122
Byzantine Empire
A: 18–19, 21, 36, 38

C

Cacafuego (ship)
B: 84
"Caesar." *See* Julius Caesar and
the Cilician Pirates
Caesar, Julius
A: 12–14, 13 (ill.)
PS: 14–19, 18 (ill.)
"Calico Jack." *See* Rackham, John
"Calico Jack"
Campeachy
B: 63
Campeche, Mexico
B: 63, 159–60, 188
Canada
A: 113, 145
copyright reform, **PS:** 208
IP piracy watch list, **PS:** 206,
208, 211, 213
pirate activity, **PS:** 80
Pirate Party, **PS:** 212
Cannibalism
B: 68, 163
Cannons
bombardment of forts,
B: 187
carrying/using on ships,
B: 4–5, 24, 58
disabling enemy cannons,
B: 127
HMS *Serapis*, **B:** 129
treasure hiding, **B:** 172
Whydah, **B:** 24–26

wounds from, **B:** 77, 188, 189, 207

See also Explosions

Canton, China
B: 53–54, 58, 60

Cape Cod, Massachusetts
B: 22, 25, 26

Cape of Good Hope
B: 99

Cape Verde Islands
B: 66, 98

Captain Blood (film, 1935)
A: 232, 232 (ill.)

Captain Blood: His Odyssey
(Sabatini)
A: 224, 231–32, 232 (ill.)

Captain Singleton (Defoe)
A: 222

"Captain Thomas." *See* Bonnet,
Stede

Captains. *See* Ships' captains;
specific captains; Adams,
Robert (captain); Antipiracy
campaigns; Bainbridge,
William; Evans, John; Flint,
Captain (literary character);
Hook, Captain (literary
character); Johnson, Charles
(captain); Phillips, Richard;
Rackham, John "Calico Jack";
Roberts, Bartholomew

Captives of pirates
Dragut Reis, **B:** 73, 76, 77
humane treatment,
B: 178–79
Henry Morgan, **B:** 167,
171 (ill.)
murder, **B:** 18, 31, 57, 117
rape, **B:** 101, 169, 185
sold as slaves, **B:** 14, 17, 57
women and children,
B: 16–17, 24, 57, 73, 76,
178, 225

Capturing ships, strategies
B: 4–5, 58, 204–5

Careening
A: 125

Caribbean, and European
colonialism
Buccaneers' era, **PS:** 51–52,
53–54, 55, 59, 60
1700s, **PS:** 89

Caribbean Sea and islands
Buccaneer activity (17th
century), **A:** 79–95, 81
(ill.), 83 (ill.), 87 (ill.)
European arrivals and
settlements,
A: 58, 78–79
golden age of piracy
(17th-18th century), **A:** 97,
98, 99, 101, 105, 106–7,
108, 109–11, 112, 117,
128, 157
Spanish Main and privateering
(16th-17th century),
A: 57–58, 59, 61–63, 63
(ill.), 66–68, 70, 71–72, 73,
77–78, 89–95

Caribbean Sea pirates
Buccaneers, **PS:** 49, 50 (ill.),
51–60
end, 18th century, **PS:** 102
totals, golden age, **PS:** 92
Welsh pirates, **PS:** 80, 85, 89

Caribbean Sea trade, and piracy
Samuel Bellamy, **B:** 21–24
Blackbeard, **B:** 29, 30
Stede Bonnet, **B:** 39
buccaneers, **B:** 158–59, 187
cannibalism, **B:** 163
William Dampier, **B:** 63–66
Francis Drake, **B:** 80–81, 83,
85–87
Henry Every, **B:** 98, 103
John Hawkins, **B:** 105,
107–8, 110, 113
Jamaica as trading base,
B: 62, 184
John Paul Jones, **B:** 124

William Kidd, **B:** 133–35,
138
Jean Lafitte, **B:** 150, 154, 156
François L'Olonnais,
B: 157–59
Henry Morgan, **B:** 165–67,
169–70, 172
Christopher Myngs,
B: 183–86, 188–90
Pirates of the Caribbean films,
B: 49
privateers, **B:** 21, 29–30, 41
Mary Read, **B:** 47–48
recruitment of pirate crews,
B: 202
Bartholomew Roberts,
B: 205–6
Woodes Rogers, **B:** 211, 215,
218
slave trade, **B:** 24, 180, 184
Spanish trade colonies,
B: 184
John Ward, **B:** 220

Caribs
PS: 49, 51, 60

Cartagena, Colombia
B: 85, 86, 152
16th century, **A:** 60, 63 (ill.)
17th century, **A:** 78, 94–95

Carthage
A: 10

Castaways. *See* Marooned sailors

Castles, Ireland
B: 192 (ill.), 193, 194–95,
196, 199

Catherine II, Empress of Russia
B: 131

Catholic Church
B: 13, 16, 73, 83, 180, 188
Catholic-Protestant conflict,
A: 61, 62–63, 85;
PS: 26, 29
Crusades, **A:** 37–38, 41;
PS: 38

Dark Ages, **A:** 19

kidnapping and theft from,
A: 21, 39, 40 (ill.)
Spanish and Dutch
monarchies, A: 72–73
Spanish and English
monarchies, A: 66, 71
Treaty of Tordesillas (1494),
A: 59, 60
See also Knights of Malta
CDs, pirated
PS: 208, 210, 211 (ill.), 213
Centurion (warship)
B: 186
Cervantes, Miguel de
A: 51, 51 (ill.)
PS: 46
Chandler, Paul
A: 189
Chandler, Rachel
A: 189, 189 (ill.)
Chang Pao
A: 169
B: 56, 59–60
PS: 109, 112, 113, 115
Chang Po Tsai. *See* Chang Pao
Channel Islands
B: 90, 91
Charitable giving
redemption of captives, A: 50
Somali pirates, A: 189–90
Victual Brothers, A: 27–28
Charles I, King of England
A: 79
B: 186
PS: 149
Charles I, King of Spain
A: 43
Charles II, King of England
A: 90–91
B: 172, 186, 188
PS: 44, 148, 149
Charles II (ship)
B: 98, 104
Charles V, King of England
B: 16, 76

Charles V, King of Spain
A: 72
Charleston, South Carolina
Blackbeard blockade,
B: 31–32, 40
Stede Bonnet, B: 37, 42
Anne Bonny, B: 46
Charlotte (English princess)
PS: 126
Chemical tankers
PS: 186
Cheng Chih Lung.
See Ching-Chi-Ling
Cheng I
A: 166–68
B: 54
PS: 107–9
Cheng I Sao
A: 166, 168, 169
B: **53–60**, 145
PS: 70, 108, 109–10,
111–14, 112 (ill.), 115
early life, B: 54
family, B: 54, 56
portrayals, B: 53 (ill.), 59 (ill.)
religious beliefs, B: 57
Cheung Son (ship)
A: 181
Child pirates
B: 23, 25
Childe Harold's Pilgrimage
(Byron)
PS: 119, 120
Children
kidnapping and slave trade,
A: 4, 79
pirates, A: 210
Chile, on IP piracy watch list
PS: 213
China
antipiracy campaigns, A: 167,
169, 180–81, 207
Beijing, B: 143
Canton, B: 53–54, 58, 60
Chang Pao, A: 167, 169

Cheng I, A: 166–68
Cheng I Sao, A: 166, 168,
169
Ching-Chi-Ling, A: 162–63
Chongzhen, Emperor, B:
142–43
Chui Apoo, A: 170, 171 (ill.)
cultural sharing values,
PS: 207, 214
end of pirate confederacy,
A: 169, 171, 177
era of pirate confederacy,
A: 166–68, 169 (ill.)
explorers and navigators,
A: 160–61
golden age of piracy, A: 157
on IP piracy watch list, PS:
205, 206, 206 (ill.), 208–9
Kho Hsing Yeh, A: 162,
163–65, 164 (ill.)
Kwangtung coast, B: 54–55
Manchus, A: 163; B: 142–44
Ming dynasty, A: 159–61,
162, 163–64; B: 141,
142–43
Nanjing, B: 142, 144
opium, B: 54–55
pirate confederations era,
B: 54–60
Qing dynasty, A: 163, 164,
165, 166, 169; B: 143, 147
sea piracy beginnings,
A: 157–58
Shap-'ng-Tsai, A: 170
Tay Son rebellion,
A: 165–66
Wokou activity, A: 158,
161–62
women pirates, A: 167, 168
See also Taiwan
Chinese naming
PS: 115
Chinese pirates
PS: 107–16, 108 (ill.)
Ching Shih. *See* Cheng I Sao

Ching-Chi-Ling
  A: 162–63
  B: 142–43
Cholera
  B: 137
Chongzhen, Emperor of China
  B: 142–43
Christian corsairs.
  See Knights of Malta;
  Renegades
Christian guidelines
  PS: 76, 77, 80
Christian-Muslim conflict
  Barbarossa pirate attacks,
    A: 39–41
  Crusades, **A:** 37–38, 41
  Knights of Malta and Barbary
    corsairs, **A:** 41–44
  Mediterranean region
    control, **A:** 35
Christians
  Christianity-Islam
    conversions, **B:** 176, 224
  conflict with Muslims, **B:** 13,
    72, 73, 77, 177, 180
  ships, raids, **B:** 11–12
  See also Catholic Church;
    Knights Hospitallers;
    Knights of Malta
Chui Apoo
  A: 170, 171 (ill.)
Cicero
  A: 7
Cilician pirates
  A: 12–14, 13 (ill.)
  PS: 14, 15–16, 17–21
Cimaroons
  A: 70
Cimarrones
  B: 81–82
Cinque Ports
  A: 28–29
Circumnavigation
  A: 70–71
  PS: 35

Francis Drake, **B:** 79, 83–85
  Woodes Rogers, **B:** 212–14
City of God (St. Augustine)
  A: 10
City-state systems
  Barbary Coast ports,
    A: 39, 44
  Greece, **A:** 4, 8–9, 10
  Italy, **A:** 21, 36, 45
Civil wars
  American, **A:** 154–55
  English, **A:** 79
  Greece, **PS:** 126
  Rome, **PS:** 14
  Somalia, **A:** 190, 203;
    PS: 179, 184, 194
Claibourne, William
  A: 152
Clairmont, Claire
  PS: 119
Clans, Somalia
  PS: 183, 185, 188
Cleopatra VII
  PS: 21
Clifford, Barry
  A: 108
  B: 25
Clothing
  A: 113, 130, 134, 158
  B: 109, 111, 204
Coast guards
  PS: 165, 183, 184, 185
Codes of conduct
  buccaneers, **A:** 85
  Cheng I Sao's fleet, **A:** 168
  See also Ships' articles
Coinage
  A: 69, 69 (ill.)
  B: 25 (ill.)
Colaba, India
  B: 7
Colombia
  B: 152
  modern piracy, **A:** 181

Christopher Myngs piracy,
  A: 90
Spanish colonialism, **A:** 60, 78
Colonial governors
  American, **A:** 103, 105, 111,
    114
  Caribbean, **A:** 109–10, 111,
    128
Colonialism
  Asia, general, **A:** 157
  England and Great Britain
    (American colonies),
    A: 100, 137–39, 141,
    142–43, 145, 146, 147
  England and Great Britain
    (Asia), **A:** 171, 172–73,
    174, 175
  England (Caribbean), **A:** 78,
    89–94, 109–10, 110–11
  France, **A:** 78, 94–95
  Netherlands, **A:** 159 (ill.),
    164–65, 173, 174
  Portugal, **A:** 59, 113, 162, 173
  Spain, **A:** 57, 58–60, 61, 63
    (ill.), 64, 67, 77–78, 89, 90,
    91, 154, 159 (ill.)
  See also Specific nations/
    regions
Columbus, Christopher
  A: 58–59
*Combat of the Giaour and the
  Hassan* (Delacroix)
  PS: 126
*Combat of the Giaour and the
  Pasha* (Delacroix)
  PS: 126
Combined Task Force 150 and
  151 (naval antipiracy forces)
  A: 206–7, 206 (ill.), 209
Communications systems,
  electronic
  PS: 195
Compensation, pirate injuries
  A: 122
  PS: 56

Computer & Communications Industry Association
PS: 211
Computer software piracy
PS: 203–4, 209, 212
Concorde (ship)
B: 39
Condent, Christopher
A: 126 (ill.)
Confederate Navy
A: 155
Confederate States of America
A: 154–55
Confederations, Chinese pirates
A: 166–68, 169
Congress, U.S.
A: 185
Congressional International Anti-Piracy Caucus
PS: 203, 204, 205–13
Conquering forces
Roman empire, **PS:** 15, 21–22
Spain, **PS:** 38–39
Conquistadors
A: 59–60
Conrad (literary character)
PS: 120–22, 121 (ill.), 123, 126, 127
Constantine I (Roman emperor)
PS: 17
Constantinople
A: 18, 24, 36, 38
Constitution of the United States
A: 150
PS: 102, 104
Contact Group on Somali Piracy (CGSP)
A: 205, 208
PS: 187
Continental Army
A: 138–39
Continental Congress
A: 140, 141, 142

Continental Congresses, First and Second (1774 and 1775)
A: 137–38
Continental Navy
A: 137, 139–40, 150
B: 126, 129, 131
battles and heroes, **A:** 147–49, 148 (ill.)
vs. privateers, **A:** 141, 142, 146
Continental/coastal shelves
PS: 159, 160
Conversions, religious
Christian/Catholic coercion, **A:** 37–38, 41–42
Christianity-to-Islam, **A:** 50, 51, 53, 231
Convoys at sea
British merchant ships, American Revolution, **A:** 145
British merchant ships, War of 1812, **A:** 151
Spanish flota system, **A:** 63–64, 63 (ill.), 65, 67, 68, 73, 77, 106
Conyngham, Gustavus
A: 147
Cook, James
PS: 144
Cook, John
B: 66, 67
Cooper, James Fenimore
A: 224
Coote, Richard
A: 103, 105
B: 136, 138, 139
Copyright infringement/violations. *See* Intellectual property piracy
Copyright violations and IP theft
A: 184–85
See also Intellectual property piracy
Cordingly, David
A: 65, 67, 119, 225, 233

Cordova, Spain
A: 37
Corporal punishment
galley slaves, **PS:** 34, 40
pirate ships' rules, **PS:** 76–77, 91, 92, 109
The Corsair (Byron)
A: 225–26
B: 225
PS: 117–28, 121 (ill.)
art inspirations, **PS:** 126, 127
excerpt from *The Corsair* (Byron), **PS:** 123–24
Corsairs. *See* Barbary corsairs
Cortés, Hernán
A: 59, 60
Costs of piracy
A: 150, 185, 194, 207, 213
Counterfeit goods
A: 184–85
See also Books, pirated; CDs, pirated; DVDs, pirated; Knockoff products; Software piracy
Country Watch List
PS: 203–15
excerpt from *2010 Country Watch List* (Congressional International Anti-Piracy Caucus), **PS:** 208–10
County Mayo, Ireland
B: 191–92, 192 (ill.), 194, 198
County Monmouth, Wales
B: 165
Courset, France
B: 89
Coxinga. *See* Kuo Hsing Yeh
Crassus (Roman general)
PS: 15
Creative commons licenses
PS: 205
Crete (Greek island)
A: 9, 10, 14
PS: 14, 19

Cricket, Mary
  A: 133
Crime syndicates
  A: 180, 184–85
  IP piracy, **PS:** 213
  Somali piracy, **PS:** 184
  Strait of Malacca piracy,
    PS: 170, 171–72
Critheis
  PS: 3
Croatia
  A: 45
Cromwell, Oliver
  A: 79, 89, 90–91
  B: 166, 186, 188
Crucifixion
  A: 14
  PS: 17, 18, 19
Cruelty
  François L'Olonnais, **B:** 157,
    160, 162 (ill.), 163
  Henry Morgan, **B:** 167
  Christopher Myngs, **B:** 185
  Bartholomew Roberts, **B:** 206
  See also Brutality; Torture
Crusades
  A: 37–38, 41
  B: 180
  PS: 38
Cuba
  PS: 55
  buccaneer raids, **A:** 91–92
  English privateering, **A:** 91–92
  French privateering, **A:** 61
  Christopher Myngs, **B:** 186–87
  Puerto del Principe,
    B: 168–69, 168 (ill.)
  Santiago de Cuba, **B:** 186
  Spanish exploration and
    colonialism, **A:** 59, 60, 63
    (ill.), 78, 91, 92
Culliford, Robert
  B: 135, 138
Curlew (ship)
  B: 47

Custom of the Coast (buccaneer
    rules)
  A: 85
Cutthroat Island (film, 1995)
  A: 233
Cyclops (literary character)
  PS: 7, 9, 10 (ill.), 11
Cygnet (ship)
  B: 66–68

D

da Gama, Vasco
  B: 4
Dammam, Arabian coast
  B: 120–21
Dampier, William
  B: 61–70, 61 (ill.)
  early life, **B:** 62
  literary career and nature
    writing, **B:** 61–62, 66–67,
    68–70
  privateering, **B:** 212
  reputation, **B:** 69–70
Danseker, Zymen.
  See Danser, Simon de
Danser, Simon de
  A: 52–53
Danziger, Siemen.
  See Danser, Simon de
Dark Ages
  A: 19
"Dark passage" (Gwin)
  PS: 169, 172–74
Darling children (literary
    characters)
  PS: 145, 145 (ill.), 148,
    152, 153, 153 (ill.),
    154
Darwin, Charles
  B: 67, 69
Davies family (*Peter Pan* story
    inspiration)
  PS: 143–44, 146–47, 154

Davis, Howell
  A: 113
  B: 203
  PS: 74–75, 84, 84 (ill.), 141
Davis, Thomas
  B: 26–27
Daynes, Jake
  PS: 212
de Berry, Charlotte
  PS: 70
De civitate dei (*City of God*;
    St. Augustine)
  A: 10
de Graaf, Laurens
  A: 89
de Grammont, Michel
  A: 88–89
de Pontis, Baron
  A: 95
de Sores, Jacques
  A: 61–63
Deane, Tom
  B: 49
Death of Sardanapalus (Delacroix)
  PS: 126
Death penalty
  A: 210
  PS: 17, 62, 65, 70, 81, 92,
    114, 138
Debtors' prisons
  B: 217
Declaration of Paris (1856)
  A: 154, 155
  PS: 103, 158
Defenses against pirates
  PS: 174, 184, 191–93,
    195–96, 197, 199, 200
  cross-country teamwork,
    A: 197, 201, 202 (ill.), 205,
    206–7, 209
  kidnapping avoidance, **A:** 47
  non-lethal security products,
    A: 207–8, 208–9
  privateer-specific, **A:** 63–65,
    103–4

resisting ship attacks, **A:** 127, 128, 202, 207–8, 208–9
security company hiring, **A:** 202, 209
Defoe, Daniel
  A: 220–22
  PS: 46, 87–88
  influence of William Dampier, **B:** 69–70
  pirate quotations, **A:** 199, 221–22
  Robinson Crusoe (novel), **A:** 224 **B:** 70, 213
Delacroix, Eugène
  PS: 126, 126 (ill.), 127
Democratic systems of pirates
  A: 85, 101, 107, 121–22, 122–23, 130–31
Denmark
  antipiracy work, **A:** 205, 210
  Vikings, **A:** 17, 22
  wars with Sweden, **A:** 26–27
Depp, Johnny
  A: 217, 234, 235 (ill.)
Deschamps, Jérémie
  PS: 52
Desertion
  A: 122, 168
Desjean, Jean-Bernard
  A: 95
Devereux, Robert
  B: 83
Devon, England
  B: 21, 97
Devshirmeh system
  B: 72
Dhows
  B: 118–19, 119 (ill.)
Diary of a Wimpy Kid (Kinney)
  PS: 205
Disease
  bubonic plague, **A:** 28
  cholera, **B:** 137
  dysentery, **B:** 87
  leprosy, **B:** 94

malaria, **B:** 206
onboard ships, **A:** 50, 119, 129
prisons, **A:** 146
scurvy, **B:** 111
yellow fever, **B:** 206
Disguises
  A: 47, 89, 103–4, 126, 180, 181
Disneyland
  A: 234
Djerba (island)
  A: 39
  B: 13, 74, 75–76
Djibouti Code of Conduct concerning the Repression of Piracy and Armed Robbery against Ships in the Western Indian Ocean and Gulf of Aden
  A: 205–6, 209
Doctorow, Cory
  PS: 205
d'Ogeron, Bertrand
  PS: 52
Don Juan (Byron)
  PS: 119, 120
Don Quixote (Cervantes)
  A: 51
  PS: 46
Doria, Andrea
  A: 41
  B: 16, 73–76
Doria, Giannettino
  B: 74–75
Doubloons
  A: 69, 69 (ill.)
Doughty, Thomas
  B: 83–84
D'Oyley, Edward
  A: 89
Dragut Reis
  A: 43–44
  B: 71–78, 71 (ill.)
  Barbarossa, and, **B:** 73–75
  Battle of Preveza (1538), **B:** 74

capture and imprisonment, **B:** 74–75
early life, **B:** 71–73
negotiations for release, **B:** 18
Drake, Francis
  A: 66, 67, 68, 70–71, 94
  B: 79–87, 79 (ill.)
  PS: 26, 35
  Alaska speculation, **B:** 84
  attack on Nombre de Dios, Panama, **B:** 82 (ill.)
  circumnavigation, **B:** 79, 83–85
  early life, **B:** 80
  fame, **B:** 79, 87
  family, **B:** 85
  privateering, **B:** 79–83, 86–87, 113
  slaving voyages with John Hawkins, **B:** 80–81, 107, 109, 111
  Spanish Armada, battles, **B:** 85–86
Drake (warship)
  B: 127, 129
Dramatic productions
  A: 102, 220, 229
  Peter Pan, **PS:** 145–46, 148, 153, 154
  poetry accompaniment, **PS:** 5
Dress
  A: 113, 130, 134, 158
  B: 109, 111, 204
Drinking
  alcohol for lack of clean water, **A:** 119, 122
  alcoholism, **A:** 122
  effect on battles, **B:** 127, 207
  English sailors, **B:** 7, 185
  William Kidd, **B:** 140
  leading to capture of pirates, **B:** 173
  literary portrayals, **PS:** 123, 124, 131, 135
  pirates, **A:** 27, 52, 133, 168

John Rackham and crew, **B:** 51

Bartholomew Roberts' ship's
    rules, **A:** 113

rowdy behavior among
    pirates, **B:** 42

rum, **B:** 185

sailors, **A:** 121

ships' articles and rules,
    PS: 75, 76 (ill.), 77, 78

songs, **A:** 228–29

John Ward, **B:** 220, 224

Drug trade
    A: 170
    B: 54–55

Drug use
    PS: 173

Dryden, John
    PS: 13

du Casse, Jean
    A: 95

Du Maurier, Daphne
    A: 224

Duchess (ship)
    B: 212

Dueling
    A: 111, 112 (ill.), 122
    PS: 86 (ill.), 87, 91, 92, 122

Blackbeard and Robert
    Maynard, **B:** 35 (ill.), 36

pirate dispute rules, **B:** 23

Mary Read, **B:** 49–50, 50 (ill.)

Woodes Rogers, **B:** 216–17

Duke (ship)
    B: 212, 213 (ill.)

Dumping, illegal
    PS: 182

Dutch. *See* Netherlands

Dutch East India Company
    A: 173

Dutch pirates and privateers

Barbary corsair converts,
    A: 52–53, 53–54

buccaneers, **A:** 87, 89

Spanish Main privateers,
    A: 57, 73–74, 79–80

Dutch Republic
    PS: 99

Dutch West Indies Company
    A: 73

Dutch-language works
    PS: 52, 53, 54 (ill.), 58

DVDs, pirated
    PS: 206 (ill.), 208, 209, 210,
    213

Dyak people
    A: 174

Dysentery
    B: 87

E

Earthquakes
    A: 95

East India Company
    B: 5 (ill.)

Asian trade, **B:** 4–7

East Indiamen, **B:** 100

William Dampier
    employment, **B:** 68

Henry Every encounters,
    B: 99–102

Persian Gulf trade, **B:** 119

Rahmah Ibn Jabir al-
    Jalahimah, **B:** 119–20

Woodes Rogers lawsuit,
    B: 214

See also Dutch East India
    Company; English East
    India Company

East Indiamen (ships)
    B: 100

Eden, Charles
    B: 33–34

Edward I, King of England
    A: 29, 30 (ill.)

Egypt
    B: 73

ancient, **A:** 3, 4, 5 (ill.)

antipiracy efforts, modern era,
    A: 205, 207, 209

Egyptian history and records
    PS: 2

Eighty Years' War (1568–1648)
    A: 73

Elizabeth I, Queen of England
    PS: 26, 28, 30, 144

Francis Drake, and, **B:** 83

John Hawkins, and, **B:** 112

Ireland policies, **B:** 191, 195

Grace O'Malley, and, **B:** 191,
    196–98, 197 (ill.)

privateering licenses, **B:** 81

slave trade support, **B:** 109

England

American colonialism, **A:**
    100, 137–39, 141, 142–43,
    145, 146, 147

antipiracy campaigns, **A:**
    28–29, 31, 33, 54, 55, 55
    (ill.), 109–10, 110–11,
    113–15, 115 (ill.)

antipiracy laws, **PS:** 61–62,
    92, 158

Asian colonialism, **A:** 171,
    172–73, 174, 175

Barbary Corsair piracy, **A:** 53

Black Death, **A:** 28

Caribbean colonialism, **A:** 78,
    89–94, 109–10, 110–11;
    PS: 51, 59, 89

Civil War, 1642-1651, **A:** 79

French wars and relations,
    PS: 97–99, 100–102, 103–4

mercenaries use and attacks,
    A: 25–26, 29

Middle Ages military
    conflicts, **A:** 25–26, 29–31

North African treaties, **PS:** 44

on-land kidnappings, **PS:** 39

privateer use, **A:** 28–33, 30
    (ill.), 57, 66–68, 68 (ill.),
    70–72, 79–80, 90–94,
    100–101, 102–3, 105, 145;
    PS: 25–26, 28, 30, 34, 35,
    53, 97–99, 100–102

Royal Navy, **A:** 33, 54, 66, 67, 72, 90, 114, 120–21, 120 (ill.), 137, 139, 140 (ill.), 141, 143, 145, 148–49, 170, 175

sailor life, **A:** 119–21, 120 (ill.)

Viking piracy, **A:** 19–21, 20 (ill.), 24, 25

See also England and Great Britian; English East India Company; Great Britain; United Kingdom; specific English pirates

England and Great Britain

Anglo-Dutch War (1652–54), **B:** 184

Anglo-Spanish War (1655–60), **B:** 166

Charles I, King, **B:** 186

Charles II, King, **B:** 172, 186, 188

Charles V, King, **B:** 16, 76

China, trade, **B:** 55

William Dampier, **B:** 68–69

Devon, **B:** 21, 97

Francis Drake, **B:** 79–81

Execution Dock, London, England, **B:** 140

Feversham, **B:** 219

France, wars, **B:** 89–96, 106, 134, 151, 212

Ireland, relations, **B:** 191, 195–98

James I, King, **B:** 220–24, 221 (ill.)

John, King, **B:** 90, 92

Netherlands, alliance, **B:** 137

Norfolk, **B:** 183

Plymouth, **B:** 105

raids, **B:** 123, 126–31

Mary Read, **B:** 47

Restoration, **B:** 186

Woodes Rogers, **B:** 212

Second Anglo-Dutch War (1665–67), **B:** 189

Somerset, **B:** 62

Spain, peace agreement, **B:** 223

Spain, rivalry, **B:** 22, 83, 105, 110

Spain, war, **B:** 85–86, 112–13, 166, 212

Tavistock, **B:** 79–80

Whitehaven, **B:** 126–28

See also Antipiracy campaigns; East India Company; Elizabeth I, Queen of England; England; Great Britain; Pardons and amnesty; Royal Navy (England)

England, Edward

A: 126 (ill.)

PS: 141

English Channel

B: 85, 89–91, 177

American Revolution action, **A:** 147

piracy, **A:** 17, 28–29, 31

Spanish-English warfare, **A:** 72

trade, **A:** 25, 28–29

English Civil War

A: 79

English East India Company

A: 103, 162, 170, 172–73, 175

See also East India Company

English Privateers Battle the Spanish at San Juan de Ulúa

PS: 25–36

except from *The Third Troublesome Voyage Made with the Jesus of Lübeck, the Minion and Four Other Ships to the Parts of Guinea and the West Indies, in the Years 1567 and 1568* (Hawkins), **PS:** 29–32

English Restoration

A: 90–91

English-Spanish relations

A: 66, 71, 91, 94

naval conflicts, **PS:** 35, 85

slave trade conflicts, **PS:** 25, 26–36, 28 (ill.), 33 (ill.)

Enriquez, Don Martín (Mexican viceroy)

PS: 27, 30, 31, 34, 35

Environmental destruction

A: 189–90

PS: 159, 179, 180 (ill.), 182, 184, 212

Epithets

PS: 7

Eris (goddess)

PS: 2

Escapes

Stede Bonnet, **B:** 42–43

Rahmah Ibn Jabir al-Jalahimah, **B:** 120

Kuo Hsing Yeh, **B:** 144

Jean Lafitte, **B:** 152–53

François L'Olonnais, **B:** 160

Murat Reis, **B:** 181

Bartholomew Roberts, **B:** 203–4

Espionage

B: 7, 112, 149

European Union Naval Force Somalia (EUNAVFOR)

A: 207, 209

Eustace the Monk

A: 25–26

B: 89–96, 93 (ill.)

early life, **B:** 89–90

piracy for England, **B:** 90–92

reputation, **B:** 93–96

siding with France, **B:** 92

Evans, John

PS: 83, 85–87, 88–92

Every, Henry

A: 101–2, 126 (ill.), 219, 220–22

B: 4, **97–104**, 97 (ill.)
PS: 87
chasing *Ganj-i-Sawai*,
    B: 102 (ill.)
early life, **B:** 98
in hiding, **B:** 103
Jolly Roger, **B:** 49
Evolution theories
    B: 67
Executions
    Aruj Barbarossa, **B:** 14
    Chinese government orders,
        B: 60
    Cilician pirates, **A:** 13–14
    crew of the *Fancy*, **B:** 103–4
    crew of the *Royal Fortune*,
        B: 208
    display of bodies, **B:** 36, 48,
        133, 140, 208
    Execution Dock, London,
        England, **B:** 140
    William Kidd, **B:** 133, 140
    Martinique governor,
        B: 205–6
    mercenary pirates and privateers,
        A: 26, 27, 53, 61, 105
    Henry Morgan, orders,
        B: 173
    pirates, **A:** 62, 102, 114–15,
        115 (ill.), 133–34, 230–31
    John Rackham, **B:** 48, 51
    Woodes Rogers, orders,
        B: 216
    slaves, **A:** 51
    Wang Zhi, **A:** 162
Exiled populations
    A: 78–79
Exploration and explorers
    B: 3–4, 61–62, 83–85, 144,
        163
    PS: 35, 144
    cannons, **B:** 101
    Cheng I Sao battles, **B:** 58
    Rahman Ibn Jabir
        al-Jalahimah, **B:** 121

Henry Morgan, **B:** 169–70
sinking of HMS *Oxford*, **B:** 172
See also Navigation and
    exploration
Explosions
Exquemelin, Alexander O.
    A: 82, 86, 87–88
    biography, **PS:** 52–53
    The Buccaneers of America,
        PS: 49, 52–60, 54 (ill.),
        58 (ill.)
    testimony critiques and com-
        plaints, **PS:** 57–58, 59–60
Extradition
    PS: 188, 189, 199, 201
Eyes in the Sky (EiS) (air patrol)
    PS: 175
Eyl, Somalia
    A: 191–92
    PS: 182, 183, 184, 185–86

F

Failed states
    A: 188, 197, 203, 204, 213
Faina (ship)
    A: 190
Fair use rules
    PS: 214
    China, **PS:** 207
    Pirate Party platform,
        PS: 212
Fairbanks, Douglas, Jr.
    A: 232–33
False identification
    PS: 172
Families of pirates
    B: 56, 144–45, 152
    PS: 63, 109, 115, 116,
        198–99
    aboard ships **A:** 167
Fancy (ship)
    A: 101
    B: 98–103

Farming. *See* Agriculture
Fateh Mohamed (ship)
    B: 100
Felonies
    PS: 62, 66–68, 69
Female pirates
    PS: 70, 71 (ill.), 112 (ill.)
    China, **A:** 166, 167, 168
    few known, **A:** 117, 133–34,
        133 (ill.)
Female prisoners
    PS: 77, 78 (ill.), 79, 110, 115
Females. *See* Women
Ferdinand, King of Spain
    A: 38
Feversham, England
    B: 219
Fiction. *See* Literary themes of
    piracy
Fighting
    among pirates, **A:** 103, 104
        (ill.), 122, 167
    duels, **PS:** 86 (ill.), 87, 91, 92
    hand-to-hand combat,
        A: 166, 172
    ships' articles and rules,
        PS: 75, 77, 78 (ill.), 79
    See also Dueling
File sharing
    A: 184
    See also Illegal downloads;
        Peer-to-peer file sharing
Films
    A: 232–36, 232 (ill.), 235
        (ill.)
    Avatar (2009), **PS:** 205
    The Black Pirate (1926),
        A: 232–33
    Blackbeard the Pirate (1952),
        A: 233
    Captain Blood (1935),
        A: 232, 232 (ill.)
    Cutthroat Island (1995),
        A: 233

Finding Neverland (2004),
    PS: 154
Hook (1991), **PS:** 146
IP piracy, **PS:** 205, 206 (ill.),
    207, 208, 209, 210, 212
Nate and Hayes (1983),
    A: 233
Peter Pan (1953), **A:** 233;
    PS: 145 (ill.), 146
Peter Pan (2003), **PS:** 146
*Pirates of the Caribbean: At
    World's End* (2007),
    PS: 115
Pirates of the Caribbean films,
    A: 69, 217, 234–36, 235
    (ill.)
Sea Hawk (1940), **A:** 232
Swashbuckler (1973), **A:** 233
Treasure Island films, **A:** 233
Finding Neverland (film, 2004)
    PS: 154
Finery worn by pirates
    B: 109, 111, 204
Firearms
    Continental Army, **A:** 138, 143
    modern piracy, **A:** 177, 183,
        190, 191, 193 (ill.), 202, 208
    pirate types, **A:** 128, 166
First Barbary War
    PS: 44, 45, 45 (ill.), 46
First Continental Congress
    (1774)
    A: 137–38
First Opium War (1839–42)
    A: 170
Fishing
    Asian pirates, **A:** 157–58, 182
    crimes against fishing vessels,
        A: 1, 145, 157, 180, 181
    illegal foreign fishing,
        Somalia, **A:** 188–89
    industry and exploitation,
        Somalia, **PS:** 179–80, 180
        (ill.), 182, 183–84, 185,
        186, 188

pirate ships, **A:** 122
rights, under United
    Nations Conference on
    the Law of the Sea,
    PS: 159, 161
Scandinavia, **A:** 22
Flags
    A: 47, 89, 103, 126–27, 126
        (ill.), 234
    Barbarossa, **B:** 14
    Columbia, **B:** 151
    Mughal emperor, **B:** 101
    pirate flags, **B:** 48–49
    ship identification, **B:** 99,
        133, 176–77, 207
    United States, **B:** 126
"Flail of the Spaniards."
    See L'Olonnais, François
Flanders. *See* Belgium;
    Netherlands
Fleets
    Cheng I and Cheng I Sao,
        PS: 108–9, 110, 111, 115
    Cilician pirates, **PS:** 17
    English, **PS:** 26–27, 29–31
    Greeks, **PS:** 119
    Roman empire, **PS:** 19
    See also Navies
Fleury, Jean
    A: 60–61
Flint, Captain (literary character)
    PS: 133, 135, 137, 141
Flogging
    A: 119, 168
    B: 42, 47, 124–25, 152, 167,
        202
Florida
    coastal attributes, **PS:** 26
    Spanish control, **PS:** 55
Flota system, Spanish
    A: 63–64, 63 (ill.), 65, 67, 68,
        73, 77, 106
    See also Spanish treasure ships
Fly, William
    A: 128

Flynn, Errol
    A: 232–33, 232 (ill.)
Food
    aid, Somalia, **A:** 190, 191,
        203–4, 207, 209
    buccanners, **A:** 80
    limited supplies on ships,
        B: 109
    onboard ships, **A:** 46, 49, 50,
        119, 121, 122, 123
    pirate trading posts, **A:** 99,
        100, 122
    raids for, **B:** 41, 57, 163
    See also Malnutrition;
        Starvation
Foot binding
    PS: 110, 115
Forester, C.S.
    A: 224
Former slaves
    buccaneers and pirates, **A:** 80,
        89, 132
    Cervantes brothers, **A:** 51, 51
        (ill.)
    Cimaroons, **A:** 70
    Piet Heyn, **A:** 73
    Jean Parisot de La Vallette,
        A: 44
Formosa
    A: 163, 164–65, 164 (ill.)
    B: 141–47
Forts
    Bahamas, **B:** 22
    buccaneers, **A:** 84–85, 84 (ill.)
    Cartagena, Colombia,
        A: 94–95
    Castillo del Morro,
        B: 186–87
    Colaba, **B:** 7
    Geriah, **B:** 8 (ill.), 9
    Irish, **B:** 193
    Khanderi, **B:** 7
    Khor Hassan, **B:** 116
    Nassau, **B:** 22
    Portobelo, Cuba, **A:** 92

Saint Elmo, **B:** 77

San Francisco de Campeche, **B:** 187

San Jeronimo, Portobelo, Panama, **B:** 169

San Lorenzo, Panama, **A:** 93–94; **B:** 170

Zeelandia, **B:** 146

Fortune (ship) **B:** 41–42, 43

Four Years' War (1552–27) **A:** 60

France

American relations, **PS:** 98, 102, 105

American Revolution role, **A:** 146–47

antipiracy campaigns, **A:** 54, 55, 203–4

Barbarossa alliance, **B:** 16

Caribbean colonialism, **A:** 78, 94–95; **PS:** 51, 52, 53, 55

Courset, **B:** 89

England, wars, **B:** 89–96, 106, 134, 151, 212

English privateer piracy, **A:** 31–32

English wars and relations, **PS:** 97–99, 100–102, 158

Louis VII, **B:** 92

mercenaries use, **A:** 26

Middle Ages military conflicts, **A:** 25–26, 29–31

navy, **A:** 95, 203–4

Normandy, **B:** 90–91

Philip II, **B:** 92

portrayals in art, **PS:** 126

privateer use, **A:** 57, 60–63, 79–80, 94–95, 141, 150

privateers, **PS:** 102–3, 105

protection negotiations, **PS:** 44

religious history, **PS:** 52

16th century military conflicts, **A:** 57, 60–61, 66

17th century military conflicts, **A:** 94–95

Spain, conflicts, **B:** 159

Viking piracy, **A:** 24, 25

See also specific French pirates

Francis (ship) **B:** 41–43

Franco-American Treaty of Alliance (1778) **A:** 147

Franklin, Benjamin **A:** 146–47, 148, 150 **B:** 126, 129

Franks **A:** 17

Freebooters **PS:** 55, 86, 88

"Freedom of the seas," and territorial boundaries **A:** 199–200

Freemasons **B:** 126

French and Indian War (1754–63) **A:** 141

French Guiana **PS:** 103

French West India Company **PS:** 51, 52, 53

Friendship (ship) **B:** 124

Frigates **A:** 125, 139

Fuel tankers **A:** 180, 188, 190, 207 **PS:** 172–74

G

Galapagos Islands **B:** 66–67

Galiots (boats) **A:** 47 **B:** 73

Galleons (ships) **A:** 64, 65 (ill.), 70, 72, 83 (ill.)

Galleys (ships) **A:** 45–47, 46 (ill.), 53

Barbarossa's fleet, **B:** 15

Christian, **B:** 12

Eustace the Monk, **B:** 90

Ottoman navy, **B:** 15

quadrireme type, **B:** 75

slaves, **B:** 12, 15, 18, 73–75

Galley slaves **A:** 47, 48, 49 (ill.), 50 **PS:** 34, 40

former slaves, **A:** 44, 73

Gallivats (boats) **B:** 4–5

Galveston, Texas **B:** 155

Gambling **A:** 122 **PS:** 75, 76 (ill.), 77, 79

Ganj-i-Sawai (ship) **B:** 97, 101–2, 102 (ill.)

Ganj-i-sawii (treasure ship) **A:** 101–2, 219

Gardiners Island (New York) **B:** 138, 139 (ill.)

Geist, Michael **PS:** 211

Gender roles **B:** 45, 52, 56

General Pickering (ship) **A:** 149

Genêt, Edmund Charles **PS:** 98

Geneva Conventions on the High Seas (1958, 1960) **PS:** 158–59

Genoa, Italy **B:** 75

George I, King of England **B:** 215

Geriah, India **B:** 8 (ill.), 9

Germanic tribes
  A: 17–18, 36
Germany
  Hanseatic League,
    A: 26–27
  Middle Ages military
    conflicts, **A:** 25, 26
  Viking piracy, **A:** 24
Gettleman, Jeffrey
  PS: 188
Ghurabs (ships)
  B: 4–5
*Giaour: A Fragment of a Turkish
  Tale* (Byron)
  PS: 126
Gibson, Charles
  B: 98
Gilbert, W.S.
  A: 220, 221 (ill.)
Glasspoole, Richard
  PS: 110
Global pirate attacks, 2010
  A: 186 (ill.), 198 (ill.),
    212–13
Global trade. *See* Maritime trade
Goa, India
  B: 4
Godolphin (ship)
  B: 6
Gods and goddesses. *See* Greek
  mythology; specific deities
Gold resources and prizes
  A: 57, 59, 60, 64–65, 68, 69
Golden age of piracy
  B: 46, 209
  PS: 61, 85, 92, 129, 144, 158
  biographies, **PS:** 73, 84, 88
  China's, **A:** 157
  defined, **A:** 97, 117, 157, 218
  end, **A:** 114–15; **PS:** 85, 97,
    117
  era literature, **A:** 97–98, 102,
    108–9, 218–25
  life aboard ship, **A:** 117–34
  nostalgia for, **A:** 217

Golden age of privateering
  PS: 97–99
Golden Eagle (schooner)
  A: 149
Golden Hind (ship)
  A: 70
  B: 84–85
Golden Nori (tanker)
  PS: 186
Goldman, William
  A: 224
Good Fortune (ship)
  B: 205
Goodlatte, Bob
  PS: 206, 207
Gordon, George, Lord Byron
  A: 225–26
  B: 225, 225 (ill.)
  PS: 118 (ill.)
  biography, **PS:** 117–19, 122,
    123, 125, 127
  The Corsair, **PS:** 117,
    120–27, 121 (ill.)
  legacy, **PS:** 119–20
Goths
  A: 17
Government enabling/usage of
  piracy
  ancient Greek privateering,
    A: 8–9
  ancient Rome, **A:** 13
  Austrian privateering, **A:** 45
  bribery and payouts, **A:**
    13–14, 29, 48, 114
  Dutch privateering, **A:** 57
  English privateering, **A:**
    29–33, 30 (ill.), 57, 66–68,
    70–72, 94, 103, 105
  failed states, **A:** 188, 197, 203,
    204, 213
  French privateering, **A:** 57,
    60–63, 79–80, 94–95
  government actions as piracy,
    A: 10

modern Asian piracy,
  A: 180, 181
pirates' attacking of state
  enemies, **PS:** 44, 59,
    95–96, 97, 99, 107
privateering (general),
  A: 62, 77
privateers use, **PS:** 25–26, 28,
  30, 34, 35, 85, 95–99, 96
  (ill.), 100–102, 103, 104,
  157–58
Rome, **PS:** 19, 21
Somalia, possibilities, **A:** 192
tribute payments, **A:** 24, 54
tributes (protection
  payment), **PS:** 38, 44–45
Government fighting of piracy.
  See Antipiracy campaigns
Gow, John
  A: 227
Gozo (island)
  B: 74, 75, 76
Grande Terre Island (Louisiana)
  B: 151–52, 153, 154, 155
Grapeshot
  A: 113–14, 127
Grappling hooks
  B: 127, 130
Great Britain
  antipiracy campaigns, **A:** 174,
    175
  antipiracy laws, **A:** 114, 134
  Asian colonialism, **PS:** 170,
    177
  Asian trade, **A:** 102–3, 170,
    172–73, 174
  French wars and relations,
    PS: 97–99, 100–102,
    103–4, 158
  imperialism/empire, **A:** 97,
    171, 172–73, 174, 175
  legislature and Members of
    Parliament, **PS:** 35, 119
  Royal Navy, **A:** 114, 115,
    120–21, 120 (ill.), 137,

139, 140 (ill.), 141, 143, 145, 148–49, 150–51, 170, 175

sailor life, **A:** 119–21, 120 (ill.)

War of 1812, **A:** 55, 150–51

See also England; England and Great Britain; United Kingdom

Great Ormond Street Hospital (London)
PS: 146

Greece
PS: 119, 122, 125, 126
See also Ancient Greece

Greece Lamenting on the Ruins of Missolonghi (Delacroix)
PS: 126

Greek language
PS: 4, 7

Greek mythology
PS: 2, 7, 9, 11

Grenados
A: 127

Guam
B: 68

Guilds
A: 26

Gujarat, India
B: 3

Gulf of Aden
A: 188, 193, 193 (ill.), 203, 205–7, 206 (ill.), 209, 210, 212–13
PS: 166 (ill.), 181, 185, 187

Gulf of Mexico
B: 149

Gulnare (literary character)
PS: 120–22, 126, 127

Gunn, Ben (literary character)
PS: 132–33, 140, 141

Gunpowder
A: 127, 138, 143, 168

Guns. *See* Firearms

Gwin, Peter

H

Hadrian (Roman emperor)
PS: 15

Hague Peace Conference (1907)
PS: 103–4, 158

Hallett, Maria
B: 22, 24, 26

Halyburton (warship)
PS: 198

Hand-to-hand combat
A: 166, 172

Hands, Israel (literary character)
PS: 133, 134, 138

Hansa (German guilds)
A: 26

Hanseatic League
A: 26–27, 28

Haraden, Jonathan
A: 149, 150

Harardhere, Somalia
A: 212

Harley, Mary
A: 133

Harne, Maharashtra, India
B: 1

Hassan, Mulei
B: 16

Hatch, Orrin
PS: 206, 207

Havana, Cuba
French privateer attack and abuse, **A:** 61–63
Spanish presence, **A:** 61, 64, 78

Hawkins, Jim (literary character)
A: 227–28
PS: 131–33, 135–38, 139 (ill.), 140, 141

Hawkins, John
A: 66–67, 68 (ill.), 72
B: **105–13**, 105 (ill.)
PS: 27 (ill.), 28 (ill.)
Battle of San Juan de Ulúa, **B:** 110, 110 (ill.)

biography, **PS:** 26–27, 34, 35
early life, **B:** 106–7
excerpt from *The Third Troublesome Voyage Made with the* Jesus of Lübeck, *the* Minion *and Four Other Ships to the Parts of Guinea and the West Indies, in the Years 1567 and 1568,* **PS:** 25, 28–32
government career, **B:** 112–13
privateering with Francis Drake, **B:** 86
slave trading, **B:** 80, 107–12

Hawkins, William
B: 80, 106

Hawley, John
A: 31

Health issues
bubonic plague, **A:** 28
onboard ships, **A:** 50, 119, 129
prisons, **A:** 146

Helen of Troy
PS: 2

Henley, W.E.
PS: 140, 141, 154

Henry III, King of England
A: 29

Henry IV, King of England
A: 31, 32

Henry VII, King of England
B: 195

Hera (goddess)
PS: 2

Herodotus
PS: 3

Heyn, Piet
A: 73–74, 74 (ill.)

Hispaniola
B: 134, 154–55, 166
PS: 49, 51, 53–54, 55
buccaneer bases and activity, **A:** 77, 80, 82, 83, 89
English attacks, **A:** 89

French colonialism, **A:** 94–95
Spanish exploration and
 colonialism, **A:** 59, 60, 63
 (ill.), 80
Historical records.
 See Biographical accounts of
 pirates; Newspaper reportage;
 Nonfiction literature
*History of the Liverpool Privateers
 and Letters of Marque with an
 Account of the Liverpool Slave
 Trade, 1744–1812*
 PS: 95
Hizir Barbarossa. *See* Barbarossa
HMS *Drake*
 B: 127, 129
HMS *Oxford*
 B: 172
HMS *Serapis*
 B: 129–31, 130 (ill.)
HMS *Swallow*
 B: 206–8, 208 (ill.)
 PS: 80, 81
HMS *Swallow vs. Royal Fortune*
 (1722)
 B: 207–8
HMS *Weymouth*
 B: 206
Hobhouse, John Cam
 PS: 119, 125
Hoffman, Dustin
 PS: 149 (ill.)
Holland. *See* Dutch pirates and
 privateers; Netherlands
Holy League
 A: 44
 B: 16, 73–74
Holy Roman Empire
 A: 72
Homer
 A: 6, 8
 PS: 4 (ill.)
 biography, **PS:** 3–5, 11
 excerpt from Book IX of *The
 Odyssey,* **PS:** 8
 The Odyssey, **PS:** 1, 2–11

Hong Kong
 A: 170, 181
Hook, Captain (literary
 character)
 A: 229–31
 PS: 141, 144, 150–52, 154
 inspirations, **PS:** 144
 portrayals, **PS:** 149 (ill.), 153
 (ill.)
Hook (film, 1991)
 PS: 146
Hornigold, Benjamin
 A: 105, 106, 107, 108,
 110–11
 B: 22–28, 30, 215–16
Hortop, Job
 PS: 34
Hostages
 bait to capture ships, **B:** 205
 crew of Eustace the Monk,
 B: 93
 crew of John Hawkins, **B:** 112
 Grace O'Malley's family,
 B: 196
 See also Kidnapping and
 prisoner-taking;
 Ransoms
"Hot pursuit"
 PS: 164–65, 166
Hughes, Victor
 PS: 102–3
Huguenots
 PS: 52
 exiled populations, **A:** 79, 84
 pirates, **A:** 61, 85
Hundred Years' War
 A: 29–30
Hunters and hunting
 A: 77, 80, 82, 83
Hunting
 B: 63, 158, 166
 PS: 49, 51, 55–56
Hurricanes
 A: 106

I

Iberian Peninsula
 A: 37, 38
**Ibn Jabir al-Jalahimah,
 Rahmah**
 B: 115–22, 115 (ill.)
 attacks on Bahrain trade,
 B: 116–17
 career, **B:** 117–21
 early life, **B:** 116
 suicide and legacy,
 B: 121–22
Iceland
 A: 54
 B: 178–79
 PS: 39
Ilanun people
 A: 174
The Iliad (Homer)
 A: 6
 PS: 4, 5
Illegal downloads
 PS: 203, 205, 207, 208, 209,
 210, 212
Illegal fishing
 A: 188–89
 PS: 179–80, 180 (ill.), 182,
 184, 185, 186, 188
Illustrating pirates
 PS: 130
Illustrations of pirates
 A: 229, 230 (ill.)
Illyrian pirates
 A: 10–11, 11 (ill.)
"I'm Not a Pirate, I'm the Saviour
 of the Sea" (Bahadur)
 PS: 179, 183–86
Images of piracy
 Blackbeard,
 B: 29, 36
 Pirates of the Caribbean films,
 B: 49
 romanticized, **B:** 218

scars on pirates, **B:** 117
See also Peter Pan (Barrie);
Robinson Crusoe (Defoe);
Treasure Island (Stevenson)
IMB. *See* International Maritime
Bureau (IMB)
IMO. *See* International Maritime
Organization (IMO)
Imperial Academy of Learning
(Nanjing, China)
B: 142
Impersonation trickery
A: 47, 89, 103–4, 126, 180,
181
Impressment
A: 120–21, 120 (ill.), 150
B: 153, 202, 202 (ill.), 220
PS: 34, 103
Inca Empire
A: 59–60
Incidents of piracy, 2010
A: 186 (ill.), 198 (ill.),
212–13
Indentured servants
B: 157–58
PS: 53
Caribbean exiles, **A:** 79, 86
writings, **A:** 82
See also Slave trade; Slaves
India
Kanhoji Angria, **A:** 171–73;
B: 1–9
Bombay, **B:** 1, 4, 5 (ill.), 6–7
England, relations, **B:**
98–102, 137–38
English piracy thefts from,
A: 98, 101–2, 219
English trade and colonial-
ism, **A:** 102–3, 170,
171–73
Geriah, **B:** 8 (ill.), 9
Goa, **B:** 4
Gujarat, **B:** 3
Harne, Maharashtra, **B:** 1
Maratha Empire, **B:** 1, 7, 8

Maratha navy, **B:** 1–2
Mughal Empire, **B:** 1, 97, 101
on IP piracy watch list
PS: 213
See also East India Company
Indian Ocean
B: 2–3, 5, 100, 133
PS: 103, 174, 180–81
Indonesia
Dutch trade, **A:** 173
instability, **A:** 183, 201–2
IP piracy watch list, **PS:** 213
piracy, **PS:** 169, 172–75, 177
Strait of Malacca piracy,
A: 173–74, 182, 183,
186–87, 186 (ill.),
200–202
Information Sharing Center
A: 201
Injury compensation
A: 122
B: 23, 152
PS: 56
Insanity
B: 157
"Inside jobs"
A: 180, 184
PS: 171–74
Insurance bonds, privateers
A: 142
Insurance, privateers
PS: 100
Insurance, shipping companies
A: 183, 201
Insurance, ships
PS: 172, 176, 181
Insurgent groups
Indonesia, **A:** 201–2
Philippines, **A:** 181
Somalia, **A:** 212
Intellectual property piracy
PS: 203–14, 206 (ill.), 211
(ill.), 212 (ill.)
Intellectual property theft
A: 184–85

International Chamber of
Commerce (ICC)
A: 200
International food aid
A: 190, 191, 203–4, 207, 209
International law.
See Maritime law
International Maritime Bureau
(IMB)
A: 185–86, 187–88, 200,
201, 202, 208
PS: 170, 174, 176, 181, 187,
188, 199
International Maritime
Organization (IMO)
A: 203, 205, 208, 209
International piracy laws
PS: 103–4, 157–67, 176,
186, 199
International Seabed Authority
PS: 167
International Talk Like a
Pirate Day
A: 236
International waters
A: 200
Internet, and IP theft
A: 184, 185
Internet downloads. *See* Illegal
downloads; Legal downloads
Internet service providers, and
piracy responsibility
PS: 208, 209, 210, 213
Interview with a Somali Pirate
PS: 179–90
excerpt from "I'm Not a
Pirate, I'm the Saviour
of the Sea" (Bahadur),
PS: 183–86
Interview with Captain Richard
Phillips
PS: 191–202
excerpt from "Captain
Richard Phillips and the
Pirates: What's Ahead for

the Vermont Captain"
(Allen), **PS:** 195–98
Investors
B: 85, 112, 136, 137
Barbary corsairs, **A:** 47
pirates and privateers, **A:** 62,
66, 100, 102, 105, 142,
146; **PS:** 26, 28, 96–97,
105, 181, 18
Somali piracy, **A:** 192
Ionian Sea
B: 15
Iran
B: 119–21
Ireland
PS: 39
Baltimore, **B:** 175, 178–80
Barbary corsair piracy,
A: 54
County Mayo, **B:** 191–92,
192 (ill.), 194, 198
English relations, **B:** 191,
195–98
Viking piracy, **A:** 20–21,
24, 25
Isabella, Queen of Spain
A: 38
Islam
conversion of captives,
B: 71–72, 176
conversion of pirates, **B:** 176,
223–24
conversions, **A:** 50, 51, 53,
231
history, **A:** 36–37
laws, and labor, **A:** 50
North Africa and Southern
Europe, **B:** 13
symbols, **B:** 14
See also Muslims; Ottoman
Empire
Islamist militants
A: 212
Istanbul, Turkey
B: 17 (ill.)

Italy
Barbary corsair piracy and
conflict,
A: 38, 44
Genoa, **B:** 75
Germanic piracy,
A: 17–18
Middle Ages commerce and
trade, **A:** 36
Naples, **B:** 16
Narentine piracy, **A:** 21
raids on, **B:** 13–14
Sicily, **B:** 13, 73–76, 180
Venice, **B:** 73, 76, 219,
220–25
Viking piracy, **A:** 24
See also Ancient Rome;
Roman Republic
iTunes
A: 185

J

Jackson, Andrew
A: 151–52
B: 153–54
Jamaica
British colonialism and
governing, **PS:** 51, 59, 62,
65–70
Buccaneer bases and activity,
A: 77, 89–90, 91, 94
capture by English forces,
B: 166, 184
William Dampier, **B:** 62
English colonialism,
A: 89–91, 94
Evans piracy, **PS:** 89, 90, 91
military use of buccaneers,
B: 189–90
Henry Morgan, **B:** 165,
172–74
Christopher Myngs, **B:** 183
pirate trials, **A:** 133–34

Spanish exploration and
colonialism, **A:** 59, 60, 63
(ill.), 89, 90, 91
trial of Anne Bonny and Mary
Read, **B:** 45
Jamaica Inn (Du Maurier)
A: 224
James I, King of England
B: 220–24, 221 (ill.)
PS: 144
Jane (ship)
B: 35–36
Janissaries
B: 72, 72 (ill.)
Ottoman navy, **B:** 76
raids, **B:** 15–16, 18
Murat Reis,
B: 180
Janszoon van Haarlem, Jan.
See Murat Reis
Japan
B: 142, 147
antipiracy efforts, **A:** 187
(ill.), 202 (ill.)
Asian trade, **A:** 64, 160, 161,
162
Wokou, **A:** 158, 161–62
Jay Treaty (1794)
PS: 98
Jean Lafitte National Historic
Park and Preserve
B: 156
Jefferson, Thomas
A: 151
PS: 44–45, 46
Jennings, Henry
A: 106
Jerusalem
A: 41–42
B: 76, 180
Jesus of Lubeck (ship)
B: 109
PS: 26, 28, 29–32, 34
Jewish pirates
B: 154

John, King of England
A: 25–26
B: 90, 92
John (ship)
B: 124
Johnson, Charles (captain)
A: 97–87, 103, 108–9, 118, 130, 133–34, 222, 223 (ill.), 224–25, 227
B: 29, 51–52, 218
PS: 73, 77, 81, 83
A General History of the Robberies and Murders of the Most Notorious Pirates,
PS: 73, 77, 83, 87, 88
excerpt from "The Life of Captain Roberts,"
PS: 78–80
identity of, **PS:** 87–88
"The Life of Captain Evans"
PS: 89–91
Johnson, Charles (playwright)
A: 102, 220
PS: 87, 88
Johnson, Samuel
A: 120
Jolly Roger
A: 126–27, 126 (ill.), 127, 234
B: 48–49
Jones, John Paul
A: 147–49, 148 (ill.)
B: 123–32, 123 (ill.)
death and burial, **B:** 130–31
disciplining crew, **B:** 124–25
early life, **B:** 123–24
quotations, **B:** 130, 130 (ill.)
raid on Earl of Selkirk, **B:** 128–29, 128 (ill.)
Journalism *See* Newspaper reportage
Juan Fernández islands
B: 212–13
Judith (ship)
B: 80–81, 110–11
PS: 32, 33, 34, 35

Julian, John
B: 26–27
Julius Caesar and the Cilician Pirates
PS: 13–23
excerpt from *Lives of Noble Grecians and Romans* (Plutarch), **PS:** 17–18
Julius Caesar (Shakespeare)
PS: 21
Jumping squirrels
PS: 170–71
Junius (Asian governor)
PS: 17, 18–19
Junks (ships)
A: 160, 160 (ill.), 163, 166, 169 (ill.)
B: 55, 143, 144, 145 (ill.)
Jurisdiction, oceans and seas
A: 198, 199–200, 205, 209–10
Jury trials
PS: 62

K

Karankawa Indians
B: 155
Katzones, Lambros
PS: 125
Kennedy, Walter
A: 126 (ill.)
B: 204
Kenyan antipiracy efforts, Somali piracy
A: 205–6, 209, 211, 211 (ill.)
Khor Hassan, Qatar
B: 116–17
Kidd, William
A: 102–5, 104 (ill.), 217, 228
B: 133–40, 133 (ill.)
PS: 141
buried treasure, **B:** 133, 138, 139 (ill.)

early life, **B:** 134
execution, **B:** 140
family, **B:** 135
influence on *Treasure Island,* **B:** 134
trial, **B:** 138–39
Kidnapping and prisoner-taking
by Kanholi Angria, **A:** 172
by Barbary corsairs, **A:** 39, 41, 47–50, 49 (ill.), 51, 53, 54
by Blackbeard, **A:** 110
by British, American Revolution, **A:** 146
by buccaneers, **A:** 92
by Narentines, **A:** 21
by privateers, **A:** 30–31
by Victual Brothers, **A:** 28
by Vikings, **A:** 19–20, 20 (ill.)
by Wokou, **A:** 158
children, for indentured servitude, **A:** 79
Chinese pirates, and on-board experiences, **PS:** 110, 111 (ill.)
Julius Caesar, by Cilician pirates, **A:** 12–14
modern African piracy, **A:** 188, 189, 189 (ill.), 190–91, 192, 205, 208
modern Asian piracy, **A:** 178, 179, 180, 183–84
rich citizens, **PS:** 14, 17
slave trade, **PS:** 14, 19, 26, 37–38, 38 (ill.), 39
slave trade, ancient world, **A:** 3–4, 12
Somali piracy, **PS:** 183, 185, 188, 191, 192–94, 195–200
Strait of Malacca piracy, **PS:** 170, 171–72
of women, modern piracy, **A:** 178, 179, 189, 189 (ill.)
See also Ransoms

Kikonians
  A: 6
  PS: 7, 8
King, John
  B: 23, 25
*The King of Pirates: Being an
  Account of the Famous
  Enterprises of Captain Avery, the
  Mock King of Madagascar*
  (pamphlet)
  A: 220–22
Kinney, Jeff
  PS: 205
Knighthood
  Francis Drake, **B:** 85
  John Hawkins, **B:** 122
  John Paul Jones, **B:** 131
  Henry Morgan, **B:** 173
  Christopher Myngs, **B:** 189
  Chaloner Ogle, **B:** 209
Knights
  A: 71, 94
Knights Hospitallers of St. John
  of Jerusalem
  A: 41, 42 (ill.)
  B: 13–16, 76, 180
Knights of Malta
  A: 41–44, 45, 177
  B: 16, 74, 76–77, 175,
    180–81
Knockoff products
  PS: 203
Knopf, Howard
  PS: 211
Korea
  A: 158, 159, 180
Koxinga. *See* Kuo Hsing Yeh
Kritzler, Edward
  B: 154
Kuna Indians
  B: 65
Kuo Hsing Yeh
  A: 162, 163–65, 164 (ill.)
  B: 141–47, 141 (ill.)

death and legacy,
  B: 146–47
early life, **B:** 142
war on the Manchus,
  B: 142–44
Kwangtung coast, China
  B: 54–55
Kwangtung province and coast,
  China
  A: 165–66, 169
Kwo Lang
  B: 58

L

La Valette, Jean Parisot de
  A: 44
Lacon, Clifford
  PS: 192
Lafitte, Jean
  A: 152–54, 153 (ill.)
  B: 149–56, 149 (ill.)
  arrest for piracy, **B:** 152
  disappearance,
    B: 155–56
  early life, **B:** 149–50
  Jewish ancestry, **B:** 154
  smuggling, **B:** 149, 150–52,
    150 (ill.), 154–55
  War of 1812, **B:** 149,
    153–54
Lafitte, Jean and Pierre
  PS: 125
Lamb, Caroline
  PS: 127
Landlocked nations, seafaring
  rights
  PS: 159, 161
Lara (Byron)
  PS: 127
Latin American piracy
  A: 154
Lawes, Nicholas
  PS: 65

Laws against piracy.
  See Antipiracy laws
Le Basque, Michel
  A: 86
Le Clerc, François
  A: 61
Lê dynasty
  A: 165
Le Grand, Pierre
  A: 82, 83 (ill.)
  PS: 57
Le Testu, Guillaume
  A: 70
  B: 81–82
Le Vasseur, Olivier
  B: 23
Legal downloads
  PS: 205
Legal trials. *See* Prosecution of
  piracy, and pirate trials
Legends and lore
  basis for modern views of
    pirates, **A:** 217–18
  Blackbeard, **B:** 29, 33, 36
  creation, oral transmission,
    A: 219
  Eustace the Monk, **A:** 26
  Henry Every, **A:** 102, 219,
    220, 222
  Kuo Hsing Yeh, **B:** 149
  Jean Lafitte, **B:** 149
  Libertalia (pirate utopia),
    A: 130–31
  Grace O'Malley, **B:** 193, 195,
    199
  shipwrecks, **B:** 26
  Klaus Störtebeker, **A:** 27
  walking the plank, **A:** 229,
    230 (ill.)
Leisler, Jacob
  B: 135
Leprosy
  B: 94
Lesbos, Greece
  B: 12

Letter from a Captive of the Corsairs
   PS: 37–47
   "Letter from Robert Adams to Captain Robert Adams" (Adams), **PS:** 42–43
Letter of Marque against the French
   PS: 95–106
   "*The Swallow*, Letter of Marque against the French, Dated 12th July 1796," **PS:** 100–103
Letters of marque
   PS: 95, 96, 96 (ill.), 97, 98, 99, 100–102, 104
   American Revolution, **A:** 141, 142, 146, 147, 150
   European vs. European powers, **A:** 29, 61, 62, 89, 91
   limitations, and evasion methods, **A:** 103–5
Letters of reprisal
   PS: 95, 99, 100–101, 104
   See also Acts of reprisal
Levasseur, François
   A: 84–85, 84 (ill.)
Lex Gabinia (Roman empire)
   PS: 19, 22
Li Ch'ang-keng
   B: 58
Libel accusations
   PS: 58 (ill.), 59
Libertalia
   A: 130–31
Liberty Leading the People (Delacroix)
   PS: 126
Liberty poles
   A: 142–43
The Life and Adventures of Capt. John Avery; the Famous English Pirate (Rais'd from a Cabbin Boy, to a King) Now in Possession of Madagascar (pamphlet)
   A: 219, 220

The Life of Captain Evans
   PS: 83–93
   "The Life of Captain Evans" (Johnson), **PS:** 89–91
"The Life of Captain Roberts." *See* Bartholomew Roberts's Ship's Articles
The Lighthouse at the end of the World (Verne)
   A: 224
Lincoln, Abraham
   A: 154
Lindisfarne, England
   A: 19–20, 20 (ill.)
Lipari (island)
   A: 41
Literacy, sailors and pirates
   B: 69
Literary portrayals of piracy
   adventure stories, **A:** 224, 227–29
   biographies, **A:** 82, 87–88, 97–98, 108–9, 118, 222–25, 223 (ill.), 227
   dramas, **A:** 102, 220, 229
   golden age writings, **A:** 102, 218–25
   illustrations, **A:** 229, 230 (ill.)
   lasting characters, **A:** 228, 229–31
   newspaper coverage, **A:** 103, 217, 218–19, 222
   nonfiction works, **A:** 82, 102, 108, 117, 118, 130–31
   romantic era, **A:** 225–27
   selected fiction, **A:** 224
   swashbucklers, **A:** 231–33, 232 (ill.)
   21st century media, **A:** 217, 233–36
Literary themes of piracy
   PS: 46, 87, 88, 117, 125, 127, 129

Lives of Noble Grecians and Romans (Plutarch)
   PS: 15, 16–17, 16 (ill.)
Livingston, Robert
   B: 136
L'Olonnais, François
   A: 86–88
   B: **157–64**, 157 (ill.)
   PS: 57
   buccaneers and, **B:** 158–63
   cruelty, **B:** 157, 160, 162 (ill.), 163
   early life, **B:** 157–58
   "Flail of the Spaniards," **B:** 159–61
Long John Silver (literary character)
   A: 227–28, 233
   PS: 132, 133, 134, 134 (ill.), 135–38, 139 (ill.), 144
Loot. *See* Booty
Lord Byron. *See* Gordon, George, Lord Byron
Lost Boys (literary characters)
   PS: 144, 148, 150, 151, 152, 153
Louis VII, King of France
   B: 92
Louisiana
   PS: 125
   See also Barataria, Louisiana; Grande Terre Island (Louisiana); New Orleans, Louisiana
Low, Edward
   A: 126 (ill.), 129
Lowther, George
   A: 129, 132
Lucretia and Catherine (ship)
   PS: 90, 91
Lukkas (sea raiders)
   A: 3, 4
Lukman (Indonesian sailor)
   PS: 172–74

Lycians (sea raiders)
  A: 3
Lyne, Philip
  A: 128

M

Macao (island)
  A: 162
Macedonian kingdom
  A: 8, 10
Machias Bay, Maine
  A: 142–43
Maciver, John
  PS: 99, 101, 102
Madagascar
  Henry Every, **B:** 99, 100, 103
  William Kidd, **B:** 137–38
  pirate base failures, **A:** 131
  Pirate Round travel, **A:** 99, 99 (ill.), 100, 101
  pirate settlement myths and stories, **A:** 102, 130–31, 219, 220–22
  Woodes Rogers, **B:** 214
Madison, James
  B: 154–55
Maersk Alabama (ship)
  A: 190–91
  PS: 191–94, 194 (ill.), 195–96, 198, 199
Magellan Star (ship)
  PS: 187 (ill.)
Magic and supernatural powers
  B: 29, 32, 94, 146–47
Maine
  A: 142–43
Malabar Coast (India)
  A: 100, 171–72
  B: 4, 6–8
Malacca Strait Patrols
  PS: 175

Malacca Strait, piracy and antipiracy campaigns
  PS: 169–77
Malaria
  B: 206
Malay Peninsula/Malaysia piracy
  A: 173–74, 182, 186, 186 (ill.), 187 (ill.), 200–202, 202 (ill.)
Malay people
  A: 174
Malaysia
  IP piracy watch list, **PS:** 206
  piracy, **PS:** 169–70, 172–76, 177
Malnutrition
  B: 68, 111, 171
Malta
  A: 43, 44
  B: 77, 180–81
Man-of-war ships, Portuguese
  B: 58
Manchuria
  B: 142
Manchus
  A: 163
  B: 142–44
Mangrove waterways
  PS: 169
Maps, treasure
  A: 227
  PS: 129, 131, 133, 139–40
Maracaibo, Venezuela
  A: 86, 92–93, 93 (ill.)
Maratha Empire
  B: 1, 7, 8
Maratha navy
  B: 1–2
Marathas
  A: 172
Marco Polo
  B: 3
Margaretta (schooner)
  A: 143

Marino Faliero Decapitated on the Giant's Staircase of the Ducal Palace (Delacroix)
  PS: 126
Maritime law
  admiralty courts, **A:** 62, 142, 145
  history and challenges, **A:** 33, 198–200
  jurisdiction, **A:** 198, 199–200, 205, 209–10
  modern world, **A:** 180, 197, 200, 201, 203, 204–6, 209–11, 212
Maritime trade
  Africa/Indian Ocean, **A:** 188, 190, 203, 207–8
  American history, **A:** 141, 150
  American Revolution, **A:** 139, 140, 142–43
  Asian continent: general, **A:** 157
  Black Death, **A:** 28
  changes, Dark Ages, **A:** 19
  English colonies, trade laws, **A:** 100, 137–38, 139
  European continent, **A:** 72
  India, **A:** 102–3, 171–73
  inter-Asian, **A:** 160, 161, 162
  Mediterranean Sea, and Barbary piracy, **A:** 35, 54–55
  Mediterranean Sea, and Christian-Muslim conflict, **A:** 35, 43
  Mediterranean Sea regions and routes, ancient world, **A:** 2–3, 3 (ill.), 4
  Mediterranean Sea regions and routes, Middle Ages, **A:** 19, 25, 28, 36
  Ming dynasty policy, **A:** 159, 161, 162

modern era, international freight, **A:** 194, 197

monopolies, Asia, **A:** 157, 163, 171, 173, 174

national and military protection, **A:** 114, 115

piracy disruption, **A:** 4, 9, 11, 12, 14, 28, 97, 102–3, 169, 174–75, 182, 194

South China Sea, **A:** 157, 162, 163, 170–71, 173

Spanish Main, **A:** 57, 60, 66–67

Strait of Malacca, **A:** 173–75, 182, 201

total worth, **A:** 194

War of 1812, **A:** 150

See also Dutch East India Company; Dutch West Indies Company; English East India Company

Marooned sailors

Stede Bonnet and crew, **B:** 41

William Dampier, **B:** 68

Henry Every crew, **B:** 103

John Hawkins crew, **B:** 111–12

William Kidd, **B:** 135

Alexander Selkirk, **B:** 213

Marooning

PS: 130–31, 133, 141

in literature, **A:** 228

as pirate punishment, **A:** 85, 122

Marston Moor (ship)

B: 184

Martial law

B: 216

Martinique

A: 128

B: 157–58, 205–6

Mary Anne (ship)

B: 23

Mary I, Queen of England

A: 66

Mary (ship)

PS: 67–68

Masons

B: 126

Massachusetts

B: 22, 25, 26, 135, 136

Massacres

B: 185

Matelotage

A: 81–82

Matelots

PS: 51, 55

Matthews, Thomas

B: 7

Maynard, Robert

A: 111, 112 (ill.)

B: 34–35, 35 (ill.), 36

McCaughrean, Geraldine

PS: 146

Media sales

PS: 205, 209, 210

Medicine as plunder

B: 31–32

Medieval European piracy

A: 17–33, 36

Mediterranean Sea

Barbarossa, **B:** 11–16, 18

Dragut Reis, **B:** 73, 77

Murat Reis, **B:** 175, 180

John Ward, **B:** 219–26

Mediterranean Sea region piracy

ancient world, **A:** 1–15, 5 (ill.), 36; **PS:** 1–2, 9

Barbary corsairs, **A:** 35–41, 36 (ill.), 40 (ill.), 43–55, 47 (ill.), 49 (ill.), 55 (ill.)

Knights of Malta, **A:** 41–44, 42 (ill.)

Middle Ages, **A:** 18–19, 21, 24, 36

Roman Empire, **PS:** 9, 13, 14, 19–21

17th–18th century North Africa, **PS:** 37, 39, 44

Medora (literary character)

PS: 120, 121 (ill.), 122, 127

Meirion, Dafydd

PS: 83–84, 92

Melesigenes. *See* Homer

Menelaus, King of Sparta

PS: 2

Mercenary piracy

A: 25–26

Mestrios Ploutarchos. *See* Plutarch

Mexico

Campeche, **B:** 63, 159–60, 188

colonialism and slave trade, **PS:** 26–27, 29–32, 34, 35, 55

IP piracy watch list, **PS:** 206, 207, 209

San Juan de Ulúa, **B:** 80, 109–10

Spanish trade colonies, **B:** 184

Meyer, L.A.

A: 224

Microsoft

PS: 204

Middle Ages

A: 17, 18–19

Middle East

Crusades, **PS:** 38

slaves, **PS:** 40

Mines, and mined treasure

A: 60, 64, 68, 69

Ming dynasty

A: 159–61, 162, 163–64

B: 141, 142–43

Mings, Christopher. *See* Myngs, Christopher

Mining rights

PS: 159, 167

Minion (ship)

B: 110–12

PS: 28, 29–32, 34, 35

Mints

A: 69

Miskito
　　B: 167
Misson, James
　　A: 131
Mist, Nathaniel
　　PS: 88
Mithridates, King of Pontus
　　A: 12
　　PS: 14
Mithridatic Wars
　　PS: 14
Modern piracy
　　A: 177, 184–85, 194, 197
　　Africa, **A:** 187–93, 189 (ill.),
　　　　193 (ill.), 203, 208,
　　　　209–14
　　Asia, **A:** 177–83, 179 (ill.),
　　　　186 (ill.)
　　combating, **A:** 185–87, 187
　　　　(ill.), 197–214, 202 (ill.),
　　　　206 (ill.)
　　intellectual piracy theft, **A:**
　　　　184–85
　　2010 incidents, **A:** 186 (ill.),
　　　　198 (ill.), 212–13
Modyford, Thomas
　　A: 91, 92, 93, 94
　　B: 167–68, 172–73, 188–89
Mogadishu, Somalia
　　A: 214
Molasses
　　B: 185
Monarchial power
　　antipiracy campaigns
　　　　(England), **A:** 28–29
　　reigning in of privateers,
　　　　A: 91
　　Spanish, and control of Spain,
　　　　A: 38
　　use of mercenaries, **A:** 25–26
　　use of privateers, **A:** 29–33,
　　　　30 (ill.), 61, 62, 66, 70,
　　　　71–72, 95
　　weakened during Dark Ages,
　　　　A: 19

Monks, Benedictine
　　B: 89, 94
Monopolies, Asian trade
　　A: 157, 163, 171, 173, 174
Moody, Christopher
　　A: 126 (ill.)
Moore, James
　　A: 143
Moore, John Robert
　　PS: 87–88
Moore, Thomas
　　PS: 127
Moore, William
　　A: 103, 104 (ill.)
　　B: 137, 138–39
Moors
　　A: 37, 38
　　PS: 38, 39
Morgan, Henry
　　A: 87 (ill.), 91–94, 93 (ill.)
　　B: **165–74**, 165 (ill.)
　　PS: 52, 54, 58, 58 (ill.),
　　　　59–60, 83
　　crew, **B:** 63, 168 (ill.)
　　cruelty, **B:** 167
　　early life, **B:** 165–66
　　political career, **B:** 173–74
　　raids on Spanish settlements,
　　　　B: 166–73
　　sacking of Panama City,
　　　　B: 171 (ill.)
　　sailing with Christopher
　　　　Myngs, **B:** 190
Morocco
　　B: 175, 177–78
　　PS: 37, 39, 40, 41–42, 46
Mosquito Coast
　　B: 162
Movies. *See* Films
Mughal Empire
　　A: 101, 102, 171–72, 173
　　B: 1, 97, 101–2, 103–4
Muhammad (prophet)
　　A: 36–37
　　B: 14

Mully Ishmael
　　PS: 40
Mumbai, India. *See* Bombay,
　　India
Murat Reis
　　A: 53–54
　　B: **175–81**
　　early life, **B:** 176
　　family, **B:** 176, 177, 179
　　imprisonment on Malta,
　　　　B: 180–81
　　joins Barbary corsairs,
　　　　B: 176–77
　　voyages to Iceland and
　　　　Ireland, **B:** 178–80
Murder trials
　　B: 138–39
Muse, Abduwali Abdukhadir
　　A: 190–91
　　PS: 193, 194, 195, 196,
　　　　198–99, 201
Music
　　aboard pirate ships,
　　　　PS: 76, 80
　　bootlegs, **PS:** 208, 210, 211
　　　　(ill.)
　　illegal file sharing and
　　　　downloading, **PS:** 203,
　　　　205, 207, 209, 210, 212
　　poetry accompaniment,
　　　　PS: 5
Music industry
　　A: 184, 185
Muslims
　　Barbarossa, **B:** 12, 14
　　Christian captives, **B:** 181
　　Christians, conflict, **B:** 13, 73,
　　　　76, 177, 180
　　Dragut Reis, **B:** 71
　　expulsion from Spain, **B:** 13
　　Murat Reis, **B:** 176, 179
　　Turkish, **B:** 12
　　See also Christian-Muslim
　　　　conflict; Islam; Islam;
　　　　Janissaries; Mughal Empire

Mutiny
  PS: 75
    captains' avoidance, **B:** 124
    Charles II, renamed *Fancy*,
      B: 98, 103, 104
    crew of *Adventure Galley*,
      B: 137
    crew of *Marston Moor*, **B:** 184
    crew of *Ranger*, **B:** 127
    Henry Every and crew, **A:** 101
    international piracy conven-
      tions, **PS:** 162
    Walter Kennedy, **B:** 204
    William Kidd, **B:** 134, 135
    literary portrayals,
      PS: 132–33, 134, 139 (ill.)
    naval vessels, **B:** 216
    punishments, **PS:** 130–31,
      141
    punishments for plotting,
      B: 83–84, 117
    threats, **A:** 103
    in *Treasure Island*, **A:** 227–28
Myngs, Christopher
  A: 90–91
  B: 183–90, 183 (ill.)
    career in Royal Navy,
      B: 183–85, 189, 189 (ill.)
    defense of Jamaica,
      B: 166–67
    embezzlement charges,
      B: 186
    Four Days Battle (1666),
      B: 189 (ill.)
    raids on Spanish ports,
      B: 183
Myths. *See* Legends and lore

N

Naifeh, Ted
  A: 224
Nana (literary character)
  PS: 146

Nancy (ship)
  A: 143
Nanjing, China
  B: 142, 144
Naples, Italy
  B: 16
Napoleon Bonaparte
  PS: 103
Napster
  A: 184, 185
Narentine people
  A: 21
Nassau, Bahamas
  A: 106–7, 108, 110–11, 112
  B: 22, 46, 126, 215, 216, 217,
    218
Nate and Hayes (film, 1983)
  A: 233
National Geographic (periodical)
  PS: 169, 172–74
Native Americans
  PS: 49, 51, 60
    French and Indian War
      (1754–63), **A:** 141
    Karankawa, **B:** 155
    Kuna, **B:** 65
    Miskito, **B:** 167
    Panama, **B:** 163
    Spanish exploitation, **A:** 57,
      59–60
NATO. *See* North Atlantic
  Treaty Organization (NATO)
Naturalists and nature writing
  B: 61–62, 66–67, 68–70
Nau, Jean-David. *See* L'Olonnais,
  François
Naval Act of 1794 (United States)
  B: 131
Navies
    antipiracy efforts and forces,
      A: 206–7, 206 (ill.), 209,
      210, 213
    Arab states, **A:** 207, 209
    Athens, **A:** 8
    Byzantine Empire, **A:** 19

China, **A:** 160, 161, 163, 167
Chinese, vs. Chinese pirates,
  PS: 110, 111, 113
Confederate (U.S. Civil
  War), **A:** 155
Continental (American
  colonies), **A:** 137, 139–40,
  141, 142, 146, 147–49,
  148 (ill.), 150
England and Great Britain,
  A: 33, 54, 66, 67, 72, 90,
  114, 115, 120–21, 120
  (ill.), 137, 139, 140 (ill.),
  141, 143, 145, 148–49,
  170, 175
English/British, **PS:** 35, 44,
  73, 85, 99, 103
European Union, **A:** 207
former pirates in, **PS:** 115
France, **A:** 95, 203–4;
  PS: 103
Illyrian kingdom, **A:** 10
impressment, **A:** 120–21, 120
  (ill.), 150
Marathas, **A:** 172
Ottoman Empire, **A:** 44
pirate fighting/capturing,
  PS: 44, 45, 45 (ill.), 46,
  64–65, 85
pirates from, **PS:** 63, 73
privateer use, **PS:** 95–97, 99,
  103, 157, 158
privateers used as/with, **A:** 27,
  29, 62
regional, Strait of Malacca,
  A: 201
Rhodes, **A:** 9
Spanish Armada, **A:** 72;
  PS: 35
United States, **A:** 54, 151,
  154, 155, 191, 206–7, 206
  (ill.); **PS:** 45, 45 (ill.), 46,
  97, 102, 103, 158, 186,
  194, 196–97, 198
Venice, **A:** 21

wages, **PS:** 105
weak/nonexistent forces, Caribbean, **A:** 57
weak/nonexistent state forces, Dark Ages, **A:** 19
See also Sailors
Navigation Acts (England) **A:** 100
Navigation and exploration
B: 68, 69, 124, 214
China, and Zheng He, **A:** 160–61
Christopher Columbus, **A:** 58
Francis Drake, **A:** 70–71
Bartholomew Roberts, **A:** 113
Spanish conquistadores, **A:** 59–60
Vikings, **A:** 23
Nepline Delima (ship) **PS:** 172–74
Netherlands
alliance with England, **B:** 137
Anglo-Dutch War (1652–54), **B:** 184
antipiracy efforts, **A:** 174, 201, 204, 207, 210
Asian colonialism, **A:** 159 (ill.), 164–65, 173, 174 **PS:** 170
Barbary corsair converts from, **A:** 52–53, 53–54
Caribbean colonialism, **A:** 78
Chinese trade and imperialism, **B:** 141, 143, 145–46, 147
Dutch Republic, provinces, **PS:** 99
18th century military conflicts, **A:** 147
Malabar Coast, **B:** 4
Middle Ages military conflicts, **A:** 25
privateer use, **A:** 57, 73–74, 79–80
privateers, **B:** 176
Mary Read, **B:** 47

Second Anglo-Dutch War (1665–67), **B:** 189
Spanish relations, **A:** 72–73, 79–80, 94
Viking piracy, **A:** 24
See also Dutch pirates and privateers
Nevis
B: 134
PS: 89
New Hampshire
B: 136
New Orleans, Louisiana
A: 151–52
B: 149, 150–51, 152, 153–54
New Providence, Bahamas
B: 22, 30–31, 39, 103, 215, 216, 217
PS: 62, 63
New York
B: 135, 136
Newfoundland, Canada
B: 62, 205
Newport, Christopher
PS: 144
Newspaper reportage
A: 103, 217, 218–19, 222
Newton, Robert
A: 233
Newydd Bach, Wales
B: 201
Ní Mhálle, Gráinne. *See* O'Malley, Grace
Nicobar Islands
B: 68
Nigerian piracy
A: 187–88
9/11. *See* September 11, 2001, terrorist attacks
Nine Years' War (1688–97)
A: 94, 100
Nombre de Dios, Panama
A: 68, 70
B: 81, 82 (ill.)

Nonfiction literature
A: 82, 102, 108, 117, 118, 130–31
Norfolk, England
B: 183
Normandy, France
B: 90–91
North African pirates. *See* Corsairs (Barbary pirates)
North America, east coast pirate activity
A: 97, 107–8, 110, 111, 113, 141
North Atlantic Treaty Organization (NATO)
A: 207, 209
PS: 185–86, 187
North Carolina (colony)
Bath, **B:** 32–34, 41
Beaufort Inlet, **B:** 32–33, 41
North Sea
antipiracy campaigns, **A:** 26
piracy, **A:** 17, 24, 28
trade, **A:** 25
Northern African coast. *See* Barbary Coast
Northern Europe
mercenary piracy and privateering, **A:** 25–28
Roman Empire influence, **A:** 17–19
Viking piracy, **A:** 19–25, 20 (ill.), 23 (ill.)
Norway
Victual Brothers piracy, **A:** 28
Vikings, **A:** 17, 22
Nostalgia
A: 217
Nueva España Flota
A: 63 (ill.), 64, 67, 73

O

Obama, Barack
PS: 197
Oberholzer-Gee, Felix
PS: 205
On Obligations (essay; Cicero)
A: 7
O'Brien, Jeremiah
A: 143
Ocean Shield (NATO)
A: 207, 209
Ocracoke Island
A: 110, 111
B: 33, 34
Odysseus (literary character)
A: 6
PS: 6–7, 6 (ill.), 8–9, 10 (ill.),
11
**Odysseus's Raid on the
Kikonians
PS: 1–12**
excerpt from Book IX of *The
Odyssey of Homer* (Homer),
PS: 8
The Odyssey (Homer)
A: 6–8
PS: 1, 2–4, 5–9, 10
(ill.), 11
Office of the U.S. Trade
Representative (USTR)
PS: 204, 208
O'Flaherty, Donal, and
O'Flaherty clan
B: 193, 194
Ogle, Chaloner
A: 113–14
B: 206–9
PS: 80–81
**O'Malley, Grace
B: 191–99**
PS: 70
arrests, B: 195–96
early life, B: 191

Elizabeth I meeting, **B:** 191,
196–98, 197 (ill.)
marriages, **B:** 193, 194–95
O'Malley castle, **B:** 192
O'Malley, Owen "Black Oak"
B: 191–93, 194
Oman
B: 120
On-land piracy
ancient Greece and Rome,
A: 8, 12
European ports, **PS:** 39
kidnapping, ancient world
slave trade, **A:** 3–4
kidnapping, Asian pirates,
A: 158
kidnapping, Barbary corsair
slave trade, **A:** 48–49, 53, 54
kidnapping, Middle Ages,
A: 21, 158
Mediterranean ports,
PS: 13, 19
Somalia jurisdiction issues,
A: 205, 214
Vikings, via rivers, **A:** 23, 24
Onslow (frigate)
PS: 77, 79
Oort, Sarah Bradley Cox
B: 135
Open sea piracy
A: 193, 212–13
Opium
A: 170
B: 54–55
trade, **PS:** 115
Oral tradition and oral poetry
PS: 4, 5
Oratory
PS: 16–17
Order of the Holy Trinity for
Redemption of Captives
A: 50, 51
Organized crime
A: 180, 184–85
PS: 213

Osbourne, Lloyd
PS: 140
Ottoman Empire
A: 36 (ill.)
PS: 37, 40, 42, 119
Balkan expansion,
A: 45
Barbarossa, **B:** 11, 13–18
Barbary corsairs, **A:** 35, 41,
44, 48
Dragut Reis,
B: 71–77
janissaries, **B:** 72
John Paul Jones,
B: 131
Mediterranean and North
African control, **A:** 35, 38,
39, 43, 44
Murat Reis, **B:** 175
navy, **B:** 15, 71, 75, 76
Ottoman Turks, **B:** 13
John Ward, **B:** 219
Ottoman Turks
A: 38
Ouidah. *See* Whydah, Benin
Overpopulation
A: 22
Oxford (ship)
B: 172

P

Pacific Ocean
B: 66–68, 79, 84–85
Pagan peoples
A: 21
Pai Ling
PS: 113
Painters
PS: 126
Pakistan, on IP piracy watch list
PS: 206, 213
Palembang, John
PS: 172–74

Pan, Peter (literary character)
  A: 229
  PS: 143, 145–46, 145 (ill.),
    151–53, 153 (ill.), 154
Panama
  A: 57, 63 (ill.), 68, 70
  PS: 54, 59
  blackmail of government,
    A: 92
  natives, **B:** 163
  Nombre de Dios, Panama,
    B: 81, 82 (ill.)
  Panama City, **B:** 170–73, 171
    (ill.)
  Panama City raid
    (1670-1671), **A:** 93–94
  Portobelo, **B:** 169
  San Lorenzo fortress, **B:** 170
  William Dampier raids,
    B: 65–66
Paradise
  A: 130–31
Pardo, Arvid
  PS: 159
Pardons and amnesty
  PS: 20, 62, 63, 112, 113,
    116, 204
  Blackbeard, **B:** 33
  Stede Bonnet, **B:** 37
  British antipiracy campaigns,
    A: 110–11
  Cheng I Sao and Chang Pao,
    B: 53, 60
  Chinese pirates, **A:** 162, 169, 170
  denials, **A:** 102, 162
  England, strategy and offers,
    B: 102, 138, 214–15
  Eustace the Monk, **B:** 92
  Jean Lafitte, **B:** 149, 153–54
  mercenary pirates, **A:** 25–26, 52
  Woodes Rogers, **B:** 211
  Roman antipiracy campaigns,
    A: 14
  John Ward, attempts,
    B: 220–24, 221 (ill.)

Paris, Prince of Troy
  PS: 2
Parrots
  B: 63
Patent infringement
  A: 184
Patent reform
  PS: 212
PATRIOT Act (2001)
  PS: 22
Paul III, Pope
  B: 16
Paul, John. *See* Jones, John Paul
Pay, Harry
  A: 31–32
Peace of Utrecht (1713)
  PS: 97
Peer-to-peer file sharing
  A: 184
  PS: 207, 210, 212, 213
Peloponnesian Wars
  A: 8
Performance bonds
  PS: 100
Perry, Mike
  PS: 192, 193, 196
Persia
  B: 119–21
Persian Gulf
  B: 115–22
Peter and Wendy (Barrie)
  A: 229
  PS: 146, 153
Peter Pan (Barrie)
  A: 229
  B: 218
  PS: 143–55
  excerpt from *Peter Pan, or The
    Boy Who Would Not Grow
    Up* (Barrie), **PS:** 150–52
  influenced by *Treasure Island*,
    PS: 141, 143, 154
  "When Wendy Grew Up: An
    Afterthought" (scene),
    PS: 146, 153

Peter Pan (film, 1953)
  A: 233
  PS: 145 (ill.), 146
Peter Pan (film, 2003)
  PS: 146
Peter Pan in Scarlet (novel;
  McCaughrean)
  PS: 146
Phantom ships
  PS: 172
Phemius
  PS: 3
Philadelphia (frigate)
  PS: 199
Philip II, King of France
  B: 92
Philip II, King of Macedonia
  A: 8
Philip II, King of Spain
  A: 66, 71–72, 72–73
  B: 112
  PS: 30, 35
Philippine Islands
  modern piracy, **A:** 181
  navigation and piracy,
    A: 174
  Spanish occupation, **A:** 64
Philips, Miles
  PS: 34
Philipse, Frederick
  A: 100
Phillips, Richard
  A: 190–91
  PS: 191–200, 192 (ill.)
Phoenicians
  A: 2–3, 3 (ill.)
Physical pirated goods. *See* Books,
  pirated; CDs, pirated; DVDs,
  pirated
Pieces of eight
  A: 69, 69 (ill.)
  B: 25, 25 (ill.), 161, 187
Piracy Act (1721)
  A: 114

Piracy as a crime. *See* Antipiracy campaigns; Antipiracy laws; Prosecution of piracy, and pirate trials; Surrender

Piracy economies
  ancient pirate havens, **A:** 9
  pirate trading posts, **A:** 100, 107
  port cities and pirate wealth, **A:** 29, 33, 38, 39, 90
  port cities and privateer wealth, **A:** 146
  Port Royal, Jamaica, **A:** 90
  Somalia, **A:** 191, 192

Piracy Reporting Centre (International Maritime Bureau)
  A: 185–86

Pirate bases
  A: 24, 25, 35, 97, 131, 163, 172
  Algiers, Algeria, **B:** 14, 177
  Bombay, India, **B:** 6
  Dammam, **B:** 120–21
  Djerba, **B:** 13, 74, 75–76
  Khor Hassan, Qatar, **B:** 116
  Nassau, Bahamas, **B:** 22, 46
  Ocracoke Island, **B:** 33, 34
  Sark (island), **B:** 91
  Tortuga, **B:** 158

Pirate codes
  Cheng I Sao, **B:** 56–57
  compensation for injuries, **B:** 23, 152
  enforcement, **B:** 57
  Jean Lafitte, **B:** 151–52
  Bartholomew Roberts, **B:** 204–5
  See also Ships' articles

Pirate councils
  A: 228

Pirate crews
  child pirates, **B:** 23, 25
  desertion, **B:** 39
  discipline, **B:** 124–25

  election of captains, **B:** 203
  recruitment, **B:** 202
  wages, **B:** 38
  See also Drinking; Mutiny

Pirate economies
  PS: 181, 182–83, 185

Pirate havens
  Bahamas, **B:** 22, 30–31, 39, 46, 103, 126, 215
  end, **A:** 15, 110–11
  England, **A:** 25, 29
  Grande Terre Island, **B:** 151–52
  Madagascar, **A:** 99, 100, 101; **B:** 99, 137–38
  Mediterranean islands, **A:** 9, 10, 12, 14, 39
  Nassau, Bahamas, **A:** 106, 107, 110–11
  Port Royal, Jamaica, **A:** 77, 89–90, 95
  Salé, Morocco, **A:** 53
  Somalia, **A:** 191–92, 205, 212
  Tortuga, **A:** 77, 80, 83–85; **B:** 159
  See also Pirate bases

Pirate hunters
  A: 134
  colonial governments, **A:** 94, 95, 109–10, 111, 114
  former pirates as, **A:** 94
  former privateers as, **A:** 110, 111
  ship captains as, **A:** 111, 112 (ill.), 113–14
  Woodes Rogers, **A:** 109–10, 111

Pirate maps
  PS: 129, 131, 133, 139–40

Pirate Party
  PS: 212, 212 (ill.)

Pirate Round
  famous pirates, **A:** 100–105, 112–14
  route, **A:** 98–100, 99 (ill.)

The Pirate (Scott)
  A: 227

Pirate Surrender Document
  PS: 107–16
  "The Pirate Surrender Document of 1810," **PS:** 113–14

Pirate vessels
  A: 123–25

Pirates Hijack a Tanker in the Strait of Malacca
  PS: 169–78

Pirates in popular culture
  A: 69, 97, 217–36

The Pirates of Panama; Or, The Buccaneers of America: A True Account of the Famous Adventures and Daring Deeds of Sir Henry Morgan and Other Notorious Freebooters of the Spanish Main. See The Buccaneers of America

The Pirates of Penzance (Gilbert and Sullivan)
  A: 220, 221 (ill.), 233

Pirates of the Caribbean films
  A: 69, 217, 234–36, 235 (ill.)
  B: 49
  PS: 115

Pizarro, Francisco
  A: 59–60

Planning, pirate attacks
  PS: 171, 171 (ill.), 181, 184, 194

Plundering
  Barbarossa, **B:** 15
  Samuel Bellamy, **B:** 21, 26
  Blackbeard, **B:** 31, 40
  Stede Bonnet, **B:** 40, 43
  Cheng I Sao, **B:** 57
  Francis Drake, **B:** 79, 81, 84–85, 87
  English coast, **B:** 223
  Henry Every, **B:** 99, 101

Rahman Ibn Jabir
al-Jalahimah, **B:** 117
William Kidd, **B:** 133,
135–40
Kuo Hsing Yeh, **B:** 142
Jean Lafitte, **B:** 155
François L'Olonnais, **B:** 161
Henry Morgan, **B:** 172
Murat Reis, **B:** 180
Christopher Myngs, **B:** 190
Grace O'Malley, **B:** 199
privateers, payments to
government, **B:** 30, 106,
134, 212
See also Booty; Treasure
Bartholomew Roberts,
B: 201, 203–4, 206
Plutarch
PS: 16 (ill.)
biography, **PS:** 15
excerpt from "Caesar,"
PS: 17–18
*Lives of Noble Grecians and
Romans*, **PS:** 15, 16–17,
16 (ill.)
Plutarch's Lives (Plutarch)
A: 12
Plymouth, England
B: 105
Poetry
A: 225–26
See also Gordon, George,
Lord Byron; Oral tradition
and oral poetry; Romantic
poets and poetry; *The
Corsair*
Political asylum
A: 210
Pollution
A: 189–90
Polly and the Pirates
(Naifeh)
A: 224
Polo, Marco
B: 3

Pompey the Great (Roman general)
A: 14–15
PS: 15, 19–21, 20 (ill.)
Pope, Roman Catholic church
A: 39, 41, 44, 59
Popular culture
A: 69, 97, 217–36
Port Royal, Jamaica
A: 77, 89–90, 91, 95
Portobelo, Cuba
A: 91–92
Portobelo, Panama
B: 169
Ports
Asian coves and lairs, **PS:** 169
Caribbean coves and lairs,
PS: 49, 51, 59
cities, kidnappings, **PS:** 13,
19, 39
French and British privateers,
PS: 98, 101, 102, 103
Portugal
African colonial areas, **A:** 113
African colonialism, **B:** 203,
207
Kanhoji Angria, peace treaty,
B: 7
Asian colonialism and trade,
A: 162, 173
Chinese trade, **B:** 55
explorers, **B:** 4
governors, **B:** 98–99
John Hawkins, encounters,
B: 107, 109
Indian trade and colonialism,
B: 4, 6, 7
trade, and relations with
Spain, **A:** 59
trade rights, Treaty of
Tordesillas, **B:** 62, 80, 158,
166, 184
Poseidon (god)
PS: 9
Potosí (South American silver source)
A: 60, 69

Prahus (canoes)
A: 174
Pregnancy
A: 134
B: 47, 51
PS: 65, 70
Press gangs
B: 202, 202 (ill.)
Prince, Lawrence
B: 24
The Princess Bride
(Goldman)
A: 224
Princess of London (ship)
PS: 73–74
Principe (Portuguese African
colony)
B: 203, 207
Pringle, Patrick
PS: 77
Prison ships
A: 146
Prisoner exchanges, pirate
PS: 193–94, 196
Prisoner exiles
A: 78–79
Prisoner-of-war status and
prisoner exchanges
American Civil War,
A: 154–55
American Revolutionary
War, **A:** 146, 147, 149
Prisoner-taking. *See* Kidnapping
and prisoner-taking
Prisoners. *See* Kidnapping and
prisoner-taking; Prisoner
exchanges, pirate; Prisoner-of-
war status and prisoner
exchange; Ransoms
Prisons
compared to sailors' lives,
A: 120
disease, **A:** 146
for Somali piracy, **A:** 210,
211, 211 (ill.), 213–14

Privacy laws
  PS: 22
Private yachts
  A: 181, 182 (ill.), 189
Privateering
  Barbarossa, **B:** 12–13
  Blackbeard, **B:** 30, 33
  Stede Bonnet, **B:** 41
  Caribbean Sea, **B:** 21
  compared to piracy, **B:** 63,
    99, 106, 134
  William Dampier, **B:** 69
  defined, **B:** 30, 80
  Francis Drake, **B:** 79–83,
    86–87, 113
  English pirates in Asia, **B:** 100
  France, **B:** 134
  John Hawkins, **B:** 106, 113
  William Kidd, **B:** 133,
    134–37
  Jean Lafitte, **B:** 152
  laws against, **B:** 223
  Murat Reis, **B:** 176
  Netherlands, **B:** 176
  Mary Read, **B:** 48
  Woodes Rogers, **B:** 212
Privateers
  A: 62
  American, **A:** 100–101, 137,
    140–47, 144 (ill.), 149–55,
    153 (ill.)**PS:** 97, 98 (ill.),
    103, 104, 158
  Ancient Greece, **A:** 8–9
  Austrian usage, **A:** 45
  blurring of privateers/pirates,
    PS: 25–26, 35, 85, 95–96,
    103, 157–58
  buccaneers' accounts, **PS:** 53
  buccaneers as, **A:** 77
  captured, accounts, **PS:** 34
  Caribbean (16th century),
    A: 57, 60–63, 66–68,
    70–74, 77–78
  Caribbean (17th century),
    A: 80, 87, 88–95

considered same as pirates,
    Ancient Greece/Rome,
    A: 7
  defenses from, **A:** 63–65,
    103–4
  Dutch usage, **A:** 57, 73–74,
    79–80
  English, **PS:** 25–36, 33 (ill.),
    53, 97–99, 100–102
  English/British usage,
    A: 28–33, 30 (ill.), 57,
    66–68, 68 (ill.), 70–72,
    79–80, 90–94, 100–101,
    102–3, 105, 145
  European end,
    A: 154
  European political conflict,
    and nations' usage,
    A: 25–28, 29–30, 57, 60,
    61, 66, 71–74, 79–80, 91,
    94–95, 105, 147, 154
  European usage and letters of
    marque, **PS:** 95–97, 96
    (ill.), 99, 100–104, 105
  French usage, **A:** 57, 60–63,
    79–80, 94–95, 141, 150
  insurance, **PS:** 100
  in Pirate Round, **A:** 100–105
  privateers-turned-pirates,
    A: 9, 25–26, 27, 29, 77, 97,
    100–101, 105, 107, 154
  Spanish usage, **A:** 141
  system, 16th century, **A:** 62
  Welsh, **PS:** 85
Prize courts
  B: 187
Prizes. See Booty
Prosecution of piracy, and pirate
  trials
  Anne Bonny, **B:** 45, 51
  Anne Bonny and Mary Read,
    PS: 65–70
  as deterrent, **PS:** 62, 92, 158
  Samuel Bellamy's crew,
    B: 26–27

Stede Bonnet, **B:**; **PS:** 187,
    188, 189, 199, 201
  British piracy crackdowns,
    A: 114
  William Every's crew, **B:** 101,
    103–4
  intellectual property piracy,
    PS: 203, 204, 208, 210
  William Kidd, **A:** 10;
    B: 138–39, 140
  modern piracy, **A:** 181, 191,
    209–11, 211 (ill.), 212,
    213–14
  John Rackham, **B:** 15
  John Rackham's crew,
    A: 133–34
  Mary Read, **B:** 45, 51
  Bartholomew Roberts' crew,
    A: 114; **PS:** 81
  Savannah's crew (U.S. Civil
    War privateering),
    A: 154–55
  Somali piracy, **B:** 3
  Strait of Malacca captures,
    PS: 174
  universal jurisdiction,
    A: 199
Prostitution
  A: 52, 81, 178
  B: 54, 194
Protection payments and
  tributes
  B: 2, 11–12, 121, 143
  PS: 38, 44–45
  Indian waters, **A:** 172
  to Barbary corsairs,
    A: 54
  to Chinese pirates, **A:** 163,
    166, 167
  to Vikings, **A:** 24
Protestants
  English, post-English Civil
    War, **A:** 89
  English-Spanish monarchy
    relations, **A:** 66, 71

Huguenots, **PS:** 52

Huguenots, and anti-Catholic violence, **A:** 61, 62–63, 85

Netherlands, **A:** 72–73

Protestant-Catholic divisions, **PS:** 26, 29

Pseudonyms **PS:** 87

Public hangings **A:** 105, 114–15, 115 (ill.), 134, 230–31

Puerto del Principe, Cuba **B:** 168–69, 168 (ill.)

Puerto Rico **A:** 59, 60, 63 (ill.)

Pyle, Howard **A:** 229, 230 (ill.) **PS:** 130

Q

Qatar **B:** 115–16, 120, 122

Qawasim **B:** 120

Qing dynasty **A:** 163, 164, 165, 166, 169 **B:** 143, 147

Qing Empire **A:** 159 (ill.)

Quadrireme galleys **B:** 75

Quartermaster duties **A:** 122, 123 **PS:** 76–77, 80

Quedah Merchant (ship) **A:** 103–4 **B:** 133, 137–39

Queen Anne's Revenge (ship) **A:** 108 **B:** 30, 32–33, 39

R

Racial stereotypes, in literature **PS:** 150, 151

Rackham, John "Calico Jack" **A:** 122–23, 133 **B:** 47, 48–49, 49 (ill.), 50–51 **PS:** 61, 62–64, 63 (ill.), 65 dress, **A:** 130, 133 Jolly Roger flag, **A:** 126 (ill.)

Radical Islamic groups **A:** 212

Raffles, Thomas Stamford **A:** 174

Raiding. *See* Attacks

Ranger (ship) **PS:** 80, 81

Ransoms **PS:** 37 Aruj Barbarossa, **B:** 12 Barbary corsair kidnappings, **A:** 47–49, 49 (ill.), 50, 51, 53 Blackbeard, **B:** 31, 40 Stede Bonnet, **B:** 40 Dragut Reis, **B:** 18, 75 encourage piracy, **PS:** 172, 196, 200 Henry Every, **B:** 99 for expected treasure, **A:** 61–62 from Chinese, **PS:** 110, 111 (ill.) from Europeans, **PS:** 37, 39, 40, 41, 43, 44, 46 from Roman citizens, **PS:** 14, 17 Julius Caesar's kidnapping by Cilicians, **A:** 12–13 François L'Olonnais, **B:** 161 Henry Morgan, **B:** 167, 169 Grace O'Malley, **B:** 194

paid for hostages, **B:** 5, 6, 40, 167, 169 for refraining from destruction/ further piracy, **A:** 86, 92, 95, 172 Bartholomew Roberts, **B:** 206 for ships, crews, and civilians, modern era, **A:** 180, 183, 184, 189, 190–91, 192, 212, 213 Somali piracy, **PS:** 180, 181, 185, 186, 196, 200 Somali pirates, **B:** 3 Strait of Malacca piracy, **PS:** 170, 172 supplies, **A:** 110 women and children, **B:** 16, 194 *See also* Bribes

Rape attempted, **B:** 46 modern piracy, **A:** 178, 179 against pirate codes, **A:** 168 rules against among pirates, **B:** 57 women captives, **B:** 101, 169, 185

Read, Mary **A:** 133, 133 (ill.), 134, 222 **B: 45–52** **PS:** 61–72, 63–70, 63 (ill.), 72 dueling, **B:** 49–50, 50 (ill.) early life, **B:** 47 fame, **B:** 51–52 family, **B:** 47 relationship with Anne Bonny, **B:** 48–49 17th century piracy, **A:** 92, 102

Read, Thomas **B:** 42

Reading and writing abilities **B:** 69

Recruitment
    American privateers vs. Navy,
        A: 141, 142
    pirates, **A:** 123, 124 (ill.), 132
Red Flag fleet
    A: 166–67, 168
    B: 56, 59
    PS: 108–9, 111, 113
The Red Rover: A Tale (Cooper)
    A: 224
Red Sea
    A: 101, 188, 193, 206, 207
    PS: 181
Reefs, destruction
    PS: 184
Reformation
    A: 72
Refugees
    Somalia, **A:** 210
    Vietnam, **A:** 177–79, 179
        (ill.)
Regional Cooperation Agreement
    on Combating Piracy and
    Armed Robbery against Ships
    in Asia (ReCAAP)
    A: 201, 205
    PS: 175
Religious centers and artifacts
    kidnapping, Narentines,
        A: 21
    looting, English privateers,
        A: 31
    looting, Victual Brothers,
        A: 28
    looting, Vikings, **A:** 19–21,
        24
Religious conversion
    Catholic conversion,
        Inquisition, **PS:** 29, 34–35
    Islamic conversion, **PS:** 39,
        40, 43
    See also Conversions,
        religious
Religious disapproval of piracy
    PS: 185, 186–87

Renegades
    A: 51–54
    PS: 39
Reneira e Soderina (ship)
    B: 220–22
*The Republic of Pirates: Being the
    True and Surprising Story of the
    Caribbean Pirates and the Man
    Who Brought Them Down*
    (Woodard)
    A: 102, 108, 220
Revenge
    A: 128
Revenge (navy ship)
    A: 147
Revenge (pirate ship)
    B: 30–32, 38–41
Rewards, pirate-fighters
    PS: 62, 92
Reza, ATM
    PS: 192, 193, 196
Rhett, William
    B: 42
Rhodes (island)
    A: 9, 42–43
    B: 13, 14, 76, 180
Right of hot pursuit
    PS: 164–65, 166
Rivers
    Barbary corsairs travel and
        piracy, **A:** 53
    buccaneer travel and piracy,
        A: 94
    mercenary pirates' usage,
        A: 26
    modern piracy, **A:** 181
    Viking travel and piracy,
        A: 23, 24
Robert, John. *See* Roberts,
    Bartholomew
Roberts, Bartholomew
    A: 112–14, 121, 128
    B: 201–9, 201 (ill.)
    PS: 74 (ill.)

    biography and ship's articles,
        PS: 73–82, 83, 84
    crew, **A:** 113, 114, 132
    death in battle, **B:** 207, 208
        (ill.)
    dress, **A:** 113, 130
    early life, **B:** 201–3
    elected captain, **B:** 203–4
    Jolly Roger flag, **A:** 126 (ill.)
    literary references, **PS:** 141,
        144, 149
    media reports, **A:** 217
    pirate code, **B:** 204–5
    ships, **A:** 113, 123
    slave abuse, **A:** 132
    success capturing ships,
        B: 205–6
    Treasure Island (Stevenson),
        B: 134
Robin Hood
    B: 95 (ill.), 96
Robinson Crusoe (Defoe)
    A: 224
    B: 70, 213
    PS: 46, 88
Rogers, Woodes
    A: 109–10, 111, 114, 131
    B: 211–18, 211 (ill.)
    PS: 62
    *A Cruising Voyage Round the
        World*, **B:** 214
    circumnavigation, **B:** 212–14
    contributions to Charles
        Johnson's work, **B:** 218
    Duke (ship), **B:** 213 (ill.)
    family, **B:** 212, 214
    governor of Bahamas,
        B: 215–16
    privateering license for Mary
        Read, **B:** 48
Roman Catholic Church.
    See Catholic Church
Roman Empire
    A: 14, 15, 17–19, 36
    expansion, **PS:** 15

piracy opposition, **PS:** 9,
19–21

political leaders, **PS:** 14–15,
17, 19

records, **PS:** 15, 19–20

Roman Republic
A: 10, 14, 15

The Romance of Eustace the Monk
(poem)
B: 90–94, 95

Romantic poets and poetry
PS: 117, 120–24, 125–27

Romantic-era pirate tales
A: 225–27

Rome. *See* Ancient Rome; Roman
Empire; Roman Republic

Ross, James
A: 175

Round ships
A: 53

Royal African Company
B: 98

Royal Fortune (ship)
B: 205–8

Royal James (ship)
B: 41–42

Royal Navy (England)
desertion, **B:** 220

William Dampier, **B:** 69

John Hawkins, **B:** 105, 112

impressment of sailors, **B:** 153,
202, 202 (ill.), 220

John Paul Jones, **B:** 124

William Kidd, rejection by,
B: 136

Henry Morgan, **B:** 166

Christopher Myngs, **B:** 183,
189

Bartholomew Roberts,
B: 203, 206–8, 208 (ill.)

Royal Rover (ship)
B: 203–4
PS: 74–75

Rules, ships. *See* Ships' articles
and rules

Rum
B: 185

Runaway slaves
B: 23, 81–82, 151, 158

Rus (Swedish Vikings)
A: 24

Russia
B: 131

exports, **PS:** 98

IP piracy watch list, **PS:** 206,
207, 210, 213

modern antipiracy efforts,
A: 207, 210

Viking piracy, **A:** 24

S

Sabatini, Rafael
A: 224, 231–33

Sabbath day
PS: 76, 77, 80

Sacking of Rome
A: 18, 36

Sagrada Familia (ship)
B: 204

Sailors
English sailor experiences,
A: 119–21

impressment, **A:** 120–21, 120
(ill.)

recruitment as pirates, **A:** 123,
124 (ill.)

transitions to piracy, **A:** 88, 98,
101, 102, 103, 105, 107–8,
117, 119, 121, 123, 128, 158

Saint Domingue
A: 95

Saint Kitts
A: 78, 79
B: 134

Salamagundi
A: 122

Sales, media
PS: 205, 209, 210

Sallee/Salé, Morocco
A: 35, 36 (ill.), 53–54
B: 175, 177–78

Salomon (ship)
B: 107

San Francisco de Campeche
B: 167, 187

San Juan de Ulúa, Mexico
B: 80, 109–10, 110 (ill.)
PS: 26–27, 29–32, 33 (ill.),
35

Battle (1567), **A:** 67, 68 (ill.)

Spanish flota travel, **A:** 64

San Lorenzo fortress, Panama
B: 170

San Pedro, Honduras
B: 161

Santiago, Cuba
French privateer attack, **A:** 61

Myngs attack, **A:** 91

Santiago de Cuba
B: 186

Santo Domingo, Hispaniola
A: 60, 61, 63 (ill.), 71, 78, 89
B: 166

Sardanapalus (Byron)
PS: 126

Saudi Arabia
B: 115

Savannah (ship)
A: *154–55*

Scandinavia
economies, **A:** 22

piracy, **A:** 27–28

wars for control, **A:** 26–27

Scandinavian pirates. *See* Rus
(Swedish Vikings); Vikings

Scars
B: 117

Schiff, Adam B.
PS: 206, 207

Schooners
A: 123, 124–25, 139, 145

Schouten, Pieter
A: 73

Scotland
> **B:** 123, 125
> pirates from, **A:** 32–33, 32 (ill.)
> Viking piracy, **A:** 20–21, 24, 25
Scott, Walter
> **A:** 225, 227
Scottish privateers
> **A:** 103
Scowerer (sloop)
> **PS:** 90
Scurvy
> **A:** 119
> **B:** 111
The Sea Cook. *See* Long John Silver (literary character)
"Sea dogs" (English 16th century privateers)
> **A:** 66–68, 70–72
Sea Hawk (film, 1940)
> **A:** 232
Sea Hawk (Sabatini)
> **A:** 231, 232
Sea people
> **A:** 3–4, 5 (ill.)
> **PS:** 1–2
Sea raiders (early pirates)
> **A:** 1, 3, 4, 7, 9
Seal of Solomon
> **B:** 14
Seamaster (boat)
> **A:** 181, 182 (ill.)
Second Anglo-Dutch War (1665–67)
> **B:** 189
Second Barbary War
> **PS:** 44, 45
Second Continental Congress (1774)
> **A:** 138
Security companies
> **A:** 202, 209
Seizures, suspected pirate ships
> **PS:** 163, 165–66, 166 (ill.)

Selkirk, Alexander
> **B:** 213
Selkirk, Earl of
> **B:** 123, 127–29, 128 (ill.)
Separatist groups
> **A:** 201–2
September 11, 2001, terrorist attacks
> **PS:** 22
Serapis (warship)
> **A:** 148–49, 148 (ill.)
> **B:** 129–31, 130 (ill.)
Seyd (literary character)
> **PS:** 120, 121–22
Shakespeare, William
> **PS:** 21
Shap-'ng-Tsai
> **A:** 170
Shared Awareness and Deconfliction (SHADE)
> **A:** 207, 209
Shark attacks
> **B:** 109
Shelley, Mary
> **PS:** 119
Shelley, Percy Bysshe
> **PS:** 119
Shih Hsiang-ku. *See* Cheng I Sao
Shih Yang. *See* Cheng I Sao
Shimo la Tewa prison
> **A:** 211, 211 (ill.)
Ship galley slaves
> **PS:** 34, 40
Shipping. *See* Maritime trade
Shipping companies
> **A:** 183, 189, 202, 207–9
Ships and shipbuilding
> **PS:** 39, 51, 56
> alterations and ship care, **A:** 125
> American colonial forces and privateers, **A:** 139–40, 144–45
> Barbary corsairs, **A:** 35, 39, 45–47, 46 (ill.), 53

buccaneers, **A:** 82, 83
China, **A:** 160, 160 (ill.), 161, 163
cogs (Hanseatic League), **A:** 26
drekars and longboats (Vikings), **A:** 19, 21, 22, 23, 23 (ill.), 24
galiots, **A:** 47
galleons (Spanish/English), **A:** 64, 65 (ill.), 70, 72, 83 (ill.)
galley ships, **A:** 45–47, 46 (ill.)
geographical centers, England, **A:** 28
junks, **A:** 160, 160 (ill.), 163, 166
pirate vessels, golden age, **A:** 123–25
prahus (canoes), **A:** 174
round ships, **A:** 53
Royal Navy (England), **A:** 139, 140 (ill.)
sagenas (Narentines), **A:** 21
speedboat use, **A:** 183, 192, 202 (ill.)
Uskok boats, **A:** 45
Ships' articles and rules
> **A:** 121–22, 132–33
> **B:** 23, 204–5
> Bartholomew Roberts' ship, **A:** 113, 12; **PS:** 75–81, 76 (ill.)
> buccaneer parties, **A:** 85, 86
> Cheng I and Cheng I Sao's confederation, **A:** 167, 168; **PS:** 109
> privateers, **A:** 142
Ships' captains
> abuse of sailors, **A:** 119, 128
> dress, **A:** 113, 130
> pirate hunters, **A:** 111, 112 (ill.), 113–14

pirate ships, **A:** 121–22, 122–23, 130

pirate victims, **A:** 175, 191

Ships of the line
A: 139, 140 (ill.)

Ships, types
baghlahs, **B:** 118
dhows, **B:** 118–19, 119 (ill.)
East Indiamen, **B:** 100
galiots, **B:** 73
ghurabs and gallivats, **B:** 4–5
junks, **B:** 55, 143, 144, 145 (ill.)
Portuguese man-of-war, **B:** 58
quadrireme galley, **B:** 75

Shipwrecks
A: 106, 107–8, 146
HMS *Oxford*, **B:** 172
François L'Olonnais, **B:** 162
Reneira e Soderina, **B:** 222
Spanish treasure ships, **B:** 22
Whydah, **B:** 25, 25 (ill.), 26
See also Artifacts

Sicily, Italy
B: 13, 73–76, 180

Siege of Rhodes (1309)
A: 42–43, 42 (ill.)

Silver resources and prizes
A: 57, 59, 60, 64, 68, 69, 70

Simeon of Durham
A: 19–20

Sinan Reis
B: 73

Singapore
A: 174, 175, 186, 186 (ill.), 201
PS: 169–70, 174, 175 (ill.)

Sirius Star (oil tanker)
A: 190
B: 3

Slave trade
Africa-Americas, **PS:** 26, 28–32, 45
American privateers, **A:** 152

Asia, **A:** 158, 174; **PS:** 169

Barbary corsairs, **A:** 41, 47, 48–50, 49 (ill.), 51, 53, 54

James Bowie, **B:** 155

Caribbean Sea, **B:** 24, 80, 184

Cilician piracy, **A:** 12

Francis Drake, **B:** 80

Dutch privateers, **A:** 73

English privateers, **A:** 66–67

Henry Every, **B:** 98, 99

golden age pirates, and black pirates, **A:** 131–32

John Hawkins, **B:** 80, 105, 107–12

indentured servants, **A:** 79

international conventions outlawing, **PS:** 159, 162, 163

John Paul Jones, **B:** 124

Knights of Malta, **A:** 43

laws against, **B:** 151

Narentine piracy, **A:** 21

North African piracy, **PS:** 37–38, 39–43, 41 (ill.), 45

pirates sold as slaves, **A:** 114

Bartholomew Roberts, **B:** 203, 206

Woodes Rogers, **B:** 214

Rome, **PS:** 13–14, 19, 21

Royal African Company, **B:** 98

Sea People piracy, **A:** 3–4

17th-18th centuries, and piracy opportunities, **A:** 98, 100, 113, 114

ship galley slaves, **PS:** 34, 40

ship living conditions, **B:** 107–8

triangular trade, **B:** 24, 106–9, 185

Wokou kidnappings, **A:** 158
See also Slaves

Slaves
buccaneer capture, **A:** 88
captives of pirates, **B:** 14, 17

captured African pirates sold as, **B:** 208

Cervantes brothers, **A:** 51, 51 (ill.)

escaped Africans, **B:** 23, 81–82, 151, 158

galley, **A:** 47, 48, 49 (ill.), 50; **B:** 12, 15, 18, 73–75

household/general labor, **A:** 49–50

janissaries, **B:** 72

women and children, **B:** 16–17, 24, 57, 73, 76, 178, 225
See also Former slaves; Slave trade

Sloops
A: 123, 124, 139

Smee (literary character)
PS: 150, 151–52

Smollett, Alexander (literary character)
PS: 132, 133, 134, 137

Smuggling
anti-smuggling campaigns, **B:** 136
Asian trade, 15th century, **A:** 161
buccaneer smuggler dealings, **A:** 80
Jean Lafitte, **A:** 152; **B:** 149, 150–52, 150 (ill.), 154–55
slaves, **A:** 73, 79

Software piracy
PS: 203–4, 209, 212

Somali piracy
A: 187, 188–93, 193 (ill.), 203, 208
B: 2–3
and Somali politics, **A:** 188, 197, 203, 204, 205, 212, 213–14
antipiracy efforts, **A:** 204–7, 206 (ill.), 210–11, 211 (ill.)

circumstances creating and
enabling piracy, **A:** 188–90,
192, 197, 203, 204 (ill.),
210, 213
prosecution of pirates,
A: 209–11, 211 (ill.),
213–14
victims, **A:** 189, 189 (ill.),
190–91, 208
Somali pirates
PS: 182 (ill.), 187 (ill.)
capture of *Maersk Alabama*
and Captain Richard
Phillips, **PS:** 191–201
interviews, pirates, **PS:** 179,
181–86
piracy creation factors,
PS: 179–81, 182–84, 185,
186, 188, 194
suspected ships, **PS:** 166 (ill.)
Somerset, England
B: 62
Songs, literary and film portrayals
A: 228–29, 236
South America
buccaneer pirating, **A:** 86,
92–93, 93 (ill.)
English privateering/exploration,
A: 70–71, 90, 92–93, 93
(ill.)
golden age pirating, **A:** 113
modern piracy, **A:** 181
Spanish Main, **A:** 57, 63 (ill.),
66–67, 78
Treaty of Tordesillas cover-
age, **A:** 59
South Asia, European colonialism
PS: 170
South Asian piracy. *See* Pirates
Hijack a Tanker in the Strait of
Malacca
South Asian tsunami, 2004
PS: 174
South Carolina (colony)
B: 37, 43

South China Sea
PS: 107–15, 170, 176
17th century view, **A:** 159
(ill.)
trade and piracy, classic era,
A: 157, 163, 167, 169,
170–71, 173, 177
trade and piracy, modern era,
A: 180
South, Thomas
B: 27
Southeast Asia. *See* Indonesia;
Malay Peninsula/Malaysia
piracy; Singapore; South China
Sea; Strait of Malacca;
Thailand and Thai piracy;
Vietnam
Spain
Anglo-Spanish War
(1655–60), **B:** 166
Armada, **B:** 85–86, 112
Asian colonialism, **A:** 64
Barbary corsair piracy and
conflict, **A:** 38, 39, 41, 44,
51, 57
Buccaneer piracy in
Caribbean, **A:** 82–83, 83
(ill.), 85, 86, 87, 88, 89,
90–94
Caribbean colonialism, **A:** 57,
58–59, 61, 63 (ill.), 67,
77–78, 89, 90, 91; **PS:** 51,
54, 55, 59, 83
Caribbean Sea, trade rights,
B: 80, 108, 158, 184
Central and South American
colonialism, **A:** 59–60, 154
Francis Drake,
B: 79–87
Dutch privateer piracy, **A:** 57,
72–74, 79–80
18th century military
conflicts, **A:** 105, 147
England, peace agreements,
B: 223

England, rivalry, **B:** 22, 83,
105, 110
England, wars, **B:** 85–86,
166, 212
English privateers and piracy,
A: 31–32, 57, 66–68, 68
(ill.), 70–72, 79–80,
90–91, 105–6
flota system, **A:** 63–64, 63
(ill.), 65, 67, 68, 73, 77,
106
French privateer piracy,
A: 57, 60–61, 79–80
Germanic piracy, **A:** 17–18
IP piracy watch list, **PS:** 206,
207, 210, 211 (ill.)
Mediterranean conquests,
PS: 38–39
Moors, **A:** 37, 38
Muslims expulsion, **B:** 176
North Africa invasion, **B:** 11,
13–14
Philip II, **B:** 112
Portugal relations, **A:** 59
privateer use, **A:** 141
privateering, **PS:** 103, 158
16th and 17th century
military conflicts, **A:** 57,
60–61, 66, 77–78, 79–80
trade rights, Treaty of
Tordesillas, **B:** 62, 80, 158,
166, 184
Viking piracy, **A:** 24
See also Spanish Main;
Spanish treasure ships
Spanish Inquisition
PS: 29, 34–35
Spanish Main
A: 63 (ill.), 77–78
origins, **A:** 58–59
privateers, **A:** 57, 60–63,
66–68, 68 (ill.), 70–74,
77–78, 89–95
riches and resources,
A: 59–60

Spanish treasure ships
   B: 21–22
   attacks on, **B:** 105, 157, 159, 161
   capture by William Dampier, **B:** 67, 69
   capture by Woodes Rogers, **B:** 213–14
   defeat of buccaneers, **B:** 67
   Portobelo, Panama, **B:** 169
   Tortuga, **B:** 158, 185
Spanish-English relations
   A: 66, 71, 91, 94
   naval conflicts, **PS:** 35, 85
   slave trade conflicts, **PS:** 25, 26–36, 28 (ill.), 33 (ill.)
Sparrow, Captain Jack (film character)
   A: 69, 217, 234, 235 (ill.)
   B: 49
Sparta (city-state)
   A: 8, 9
Speech of pirates
   catch phrases, **A:** 69, 217
   imitation, **A:** 236
   literary characters, **A:** 228
Speeches and oratory
   Samuel Bellamy, **A:** 107, 108
   Julius Caesar, **A:** 12
   James Mission, **A:** 131
   at public hangings, **A:** 114
Speedboats
   A: 183, 192, 202 (ill.)
Spies
   B: 7, 112, 149
Spotswood, Alexander
   A: 111, 114
   B: 34
St. John (ship)
   PS: 53
Starvation
   B: 111–12, 154, 171, 217
State and territorial waters
   PS: 158, 159, 160, 164–65, 166–67, 176, 186

Statehood
   A: 198–99
Stevenson, Robert Louis
   A: 69, 224, 227–28
   B: 134, 218
   PS: 132 (ill.)
   biography, **PS:** 129, 131, 154
   Treasure Island, **PS:** 129–42
   works, **PS:** 131, 140
Stockholm, Sweden
   A: 27
Storage, ships
   A: 12, 125, 163
Storms
   Cheng I, death, **B:** 56
   damage to ships, **B:** 26, 80, 103, 222
   William Dampier, **B:** 66
   hurricanes, **B:** 155
   John Paul Jones, **B:** 129
   Spanish Armada, **B:** 86
Störtebeker, Klaus
   A: 27
Strait of Magellan
   B: 84
Strait of Malacca
   A: 159 (ill.), 182
   antipiracy efforts and successes, **A:** 185–87, 201–3, 202 (ill.);
   PS: 169–77
   modern piracy, **A:** 182–87, 186 (ill.), 200–201;
   PS: 169–77
   17th- and 18th-century piracy, **A:** 173–75
Strumpf, Koleman
   PS: 205
Stuart Dynasty
   PS: 148–49
Style, John
   A: 87
The Successful Pyrate (Johnson)
   A: 102, 220

Suetonius (Roman author)
   PS: 15
Sugar crop farming
   A: 79
Suharto
   A: 183
Suleiman I, Sultan
   B: 14
Sulla (Roman dictator)
   PS: 14–15, 19
Sullivan, Arthur
   A: 220, 221 (ill.)
Sultana (ship)
   B: 23
Sumatra
   PS: 169
Sunken treasure
   A: 106, 107
Supernatural powers. *See* Magic and supernatural powers
Surcouf, Robert
   PS: 103, 104 (ill.)
Surrender
   Cheng I Sao and fleet, **PS:** 112–15
   merchant or other non-pirate ships, **A:** 82, 127
   Muse, Abduwali Abdukhadir, **PS:** 198–99
   pirate amnesty, **PS:** 20, 62, 63, 112, 113
   pirates, for pardons, **A:** 14, 110–11
   Bartholomew Roberts's crew, **PS:** 81
   towns, **A:** 21, 41, 95
Surrender documents. *See* Pirate Surrender Document
Swallow (ship, captained by Maciver)
   PS: 95, 99, 100–102
Swallow (ship, captained by Ogle)
   B: 206–8, 208 (ill.)
   PS: 80, 81

Swan, Charles
B: 66, 68
Swashbuckler (film, 1973)
A: 233
Swashbucklers
A: 221–33, 232 (ill.)
Sweden
Pirate Party, **PS:** 212
pirates, **PS:** 70, 71 (ill.), 92
Victual Brothers piracy,
A: 27–28
Vikings, **A:** 17, 22, 24
wars with Denmark,
A: 26–27
Symson, David
PS: 77
Syria
A: 4

T

Taiwan
A: 159 (ill.), 164 (ill.), 165
B: 141–47
Tanker ships
A: 180, 188, 190, 207
Tavistock, England
B: 79–80
Taxes
PS: 182, 184
Tay Son Rebellion (1771–1802)
A: 165–66
PS: 107
Teach, Edward. *See* Blackbeard
Technology tools
A: 177, 184
Telemachus (literary character)
PS: 7
Television coverage and reporting
PS: 191
Television series
A: 233
ten Hoorn, Jan
PS: 58

Tenochtitlán
A: 59, 60
Territorial and state waters
A: 199–200, 201, 203, 204–6
PS: 158, 159, 160, 164–65,
166–67, 176, 186
"Terror of the Gulf." *See* Ibn Jabir
al-Jalahimah, Rahmah
Teuta, Queen of Illyria
A: 10–11, 11 (ill.)
Tew, Thomas
A: 100–101
Texas
B: 155
Thailand and Thai piracy
A: 178–79, 179 (ill.), 180,
187 (ill.), 202 (ill.)
Thailand, on IP piracy watch list
PS: 206, 213
Thetis (goddess)
PS: 2
*The Third Troublesome Voyage
Made with the* Jesus of Lübeck,
the Minion *and Four Other
Ships to the Parts of Guinea and
the West Indies, in the Years
1567 and 1568* (Hawkins)
PS: 25, 27–32
Thorvaldsen, Bertel
PS: 119–20
Thucydides
A: 6–8
Tierra Firma Flota
A: 63 (ill.), 64, 68, 73
Tiger Lily (literary character)
PS: 146, 149–50, 151, 152
Tinker Bell (literary character)
PS: 146, 148, 152
"To a Lady Weeping," (Byron)
PS: 125–26
Tobago
B: 125
Tomato Garden (Chinese
company)
PS: 203–4

Tortuga (island and pirate haven)
A: 77, 80, 81, 82, 83–85, 84
(ill.), 89
B: 63, 158–59, 185
PS: 49, 51–52, 53–54, 55
Torture
Barbarossa's pillaging of
Lipari, **A:** 41
by buccaneers, **A:** 86, 87–88,
87 (ill.), 91, 92
William Dampier, opposition
to, **B:** 67
Henry Every and crew, **B:** 101
Knights of Malta, **B:** 175
François L'Olonnais,
B: 160–63, 162 (ill.)
Henry Morgan, **B:** 167, 169
Murat Reis, **B:** 181
Christopher Myngs, **B:** 185
Bartholomew Roberts, **B:** 206
in ship raids, **A:** 48, 101–2,
127, 128, 129, 175, 219
See also Brutality; Cruelty;
Rape
Toxic waste dumping
PS: 182
Trade routes
Arabian Sea, **B:** 3–4
Atlantic, **B:** 24, 107–9, 178
Bahamas, **B:** 22
Brazil, **B:** 203
Caribbean Sea, **B:** 46, 105,
150, 158
China, **B:** 55, 141, 143
English Channel, **B:** 90–91
Gulf of Mexico, **B:** 149
Indian Ocean, **B:** 100, 137
Ireland, **B:** 191
Kwangtung coast, China,
B: 54–55
Madagascar, **B:** 99
Malabar Coast, **B:** 4
Mediterranean Sea, **B:** 18, 73,
220–22, 224
North America, **B:** 29, 205

Persian Gulf, **B:** 119

West Africa, **B:** 201

See also Slave trade

Trademarks

   A: 184, 185

Trading markets

   pirate posts, **A:** 100, 107

   seaports, **A:** 3, 3 (ill.)

   slave trade posts,

     A: 100

   smuggling bases, **A:** 161

   See also Maritime trade

Transcript of Bonny and Read's

   Trial

   PS: 65–70

Transitional Federal Government

   (TFG), Somalia

   A: 203, 205, 210, 212, 214

Transpacific voyages

   William Dampier, **B:** 67–68

   Francis Drake, **B:** 79, 84–85

Travel and nature writing

   B: 62–63, 66–67, 68–70

Treasure

   Americas, **B:** 166

   buried, **B:** 133, 138, 139 (ill.)

   Ganj-i-Sawai, **B:** 97–98, 101

   pieces of eight, **B:** 25, 25 (ill.),

     161, 187

   shipwrecks, **B:** 22, 25, 25 (ill.)

   Spanish, **B:** 22, 81–83, 105

   See also Booty; Booty; Spanish

     treasure ships

Treasure Island (Stevenson)

   B: 134, 218

   PS: 129–42, 136 (ill.)

   excerpts from *Treasure Island*

     (Stevenson), **PS:** 135–38

   films, **A:** 233

   novel, **A:** 69, 224, 227–29

   Peter Pan influences, **PS:** 141,

     143, 154

Treasure maps

   A: 227

Treaty of Alliance with France

   (1778)

   PS: 105

Treaty of Amiens (1802)

   PS: 103

Treaty of Tordesillas (1494)

   A: 59, 60

   B: 62, 80, 158, 166, 184

Treaty of Tripoli

   PS: 45

Trengrove, Elizabeth

   PS: 77

The Trial of Anne Bonny and

   Mary Read

   PS: 61–72

   excerpt from "Transcript of

     Bonny and Read's Trial,"

     PS: 65–70

Trials. *See* Prosecution of piracy,

   and pirate trials

Triangular trade (slave trade)

   A: 66–67, 73, 79 *See also* Slave

     trade

Tributes (protection payments)

   B: 2, 11–12, 121, 143

   PS: 38, 44–45

   Indian waters, **A:** 172

   to Barbary corsairs, **A:** 54

   to Chinese pirates, **A:** 163,

     166, 167

   to Vikings, **A:** 24

Trickery

   Eustace the Monk, **B:** 94–96

   John Hawkins, **B:** 112

   Robin Hood, **B:** 95

   Henry Morgan, **B:** 170

Trilateral Coordinated Patrol

   (Malaysia, Indonesia,

   Singapore)

   PS: 174, 175, 175 (ill.)

Tripoli, Africa

   A: 35, 36 (ill.), 43, 44, 54–55

   B: 71, 76

Trojan Horse

   PS: 2

Trojan War

   A: 6

   PS: 2–3, 5–7

Trott, Nicholas

   B: 43

The Tryals of Captain John

   Rackham and other

   Pirates

   PS: 61, 64 (ill.), 65

Tsunamis

   PS: 174

Tucker, Robert

   B: 41–42

Tunis (port city)

   A: 35, 36 (ill.), 39, 44, 52–53,

     55

   B: 16, 219–20, 222,

     224–25

Turgut Reis. *See* Dragut Reis

Turkey

   B: 12, 17 (ill.), 71

Turley, Hans

   A: 225

Turner, John

   PS: 110

2010 Country Watch List.

   See Country Watch List

20th and 21st-century piracy.

   See Modern piracy

Tyrrhenian Sea

   B: 75, 77

Tz'eun Mao Szun

   B: 58

U

UNCLOS. *See* United Nations

   Convention on the Law of

   the Sea

United Colonies. *See* American

   colonies

United Kingdom

   antipiracy work, **A:** 205, 211

   ransoms policy, **A:** 189

United Nations
    Contact Group on Somali
      Piracy (CGSP), **A:** 205,
      208
    Convention on the Law of the
      Sea (UNCLOS), **A:** 200
    High Commissioner for
      Refugees, **A:** 178–79
    Office on Drugs and Crime
      (UNODC), **A:** 211
    Security Council, and
      resolutions, **A:** 204, 205,
      208, 210–11
    "UN Member States Debate
      Ways to Fight Piracy off
      Somalia" (report),
      A: 213
    World Food Programme
      (WFP), **A:** 190, 203–4
United Nations Convention on
the Law of the Sea
    PS: 157–68, 176
    excerpt from *United Nations*
      Convention on the Law of
      the Sea, **PS:** 160–65
United States
    antipiracy campaigns,
      A: 54–55, 154, 206–7, 206
      (ill.), 209
    Barbary wars, **B:** 18
    Civil War, **A:** 154–55
    consumer of pirated goods,
      PS: 207, 212–13
    English relations and trade,
      PS: 98
    French relations, **PS:** 98, 102,
      105
    Navy, **A:** 54, 151, 154, 155,
      191, 206–7, 206 (ill.);
      B: 123, 131
    New Orleans, Louisiana,
      B: 149, 150–51, 152,
      153–54
    pirate activity, **PS:** 44
    privacy laws, **PS:** 22

privateer activity, **PS:** 102,
    105, 158
Spain, relations, **B:** 155
War of 1812, **B:** 149,
    153–54, 202
See also American Revolution;
    Continental
    Navy; Massachusetts; New
    York; North Carolina
    (colony); South Carolina
    (colony); Texas; Virginia
    (colony); American
    colonies
Unity (ship)
    A: 143
U.S. Congressional International
    Anti-Piracy Caucus
    A: 185
U.S. Copyright Office
    PS: 203
U.S. Marine Corps
    PS: 46, 187 (ill.)
U.S. Navy
    PS: 45, 45 (ill.), 46, 97, 102,
      103, 158, 186, 194,
      196–97, 198
U.S. Patent Office
    PS: 203
U.S. Treasury Department
    PS: 188
Uskoks
    A: 45
USS *Alfred*
    B: 126
USS *Bainbridge*
    PS: 194, 196–97, 198,
      200 (ill.)
USS *Halyburton*
    PS: 198
USS *Providence*
    B: 126
USS *Ranger*
    B: 126–29
Utopias
    A: 130–31

V

van Haarlem, Jan Janszoon
    A: 53–54
van Hoom, Nicolas
    A: 89
Vandals
    A: 17
Vane, Charles
    A: 105, 111, 122–23,
      129
    B: 215–16
Vaughan, Lord
    B: 173
Venezuela
    John Hawkins piracy,
      A: 66
    IP piracy watch list,
      PS: 213
    François L'Olonnais piracy,
      A: 86
    modern piracy, **A:** 181
    Christopher Myngs piracy,
      A: 90
    Spanish Main, **PS:** 55, 59
Venice (city-state)
    A: 21, 36, 44, 45
Venice, Italy
    B: 73, 76, 219, 220–25
Veracruz, Mexico
    A: 78, 89
    See also San Juan de Ulúa,
      Mexico
Verdi, Giuseppe
    A: 226
Vermin
    A: 119
Verne, Jules
    A: 224
Victual Brothers
    A: 26–28
Vietnam
    B: 54
    PS: 107

boat people and modern
   piracy, **A:** 177–79, 179 (ill.)
South China Sea piracy,
   A: 159, 165–66
Vietnam War
   A: 177
Vikings
   A: 17, 22–24
   British Isles piracy, **A:** 19–21,
      20 (ill.)
   seamanship, **A:** 23–24, 23
      (ill.)
   settlements and assimilation,
      A: 22, 24, 25
   ships, **A:** 19, 21, 22, 23, 23
      (ill.), 24
Virginia (colony)
   B: 34, 36, 66, 125
Visual artists
   PS: 126, 127
Visual portrayals of piracy.
   See Images of piracy
Vosquon, Jules
   B: 47
Voting
   A: 101, 107, 108, 121,
      122–23, 131
Voyages and Descriptions
   (Dampier)
   B: 68

W

Wahhabis
   B: 115, 117, 120
Wales
   PS: 83–84, 85, 92
   County Monmouth, **B:** 165
   Newydd Bach, **B:** 201
Walking the plank
   A: 229, 230 (ill.)
   PS: 129, 131, 153 (ill.)
Wang Zhi
   A: 161–62

War of 1812
   A: 55, 150–51, 151, 152–54,
      153 (ill.)
   B: 149, 153–54, 202
   PS: 103, 105
War of the Spanish Succession
   (1701–1714)
   A: 105
Ward, John
   A: 52
   B: 219–26
   conversion to Islam,
      B: 223–24
   early life, **B:** 219
   impressment in English Royal
      Navy, **B:** 220
   later life,
      B: 225–26
Warships
   American, **A:** 139–40
   declaring, **PS:** 103–4, 158,
      160, 161
   English merchant ships
      protection, **A:** 145
   Royal Navy (England),
      A: 139, 140 (ill.), 145,
      148–49, 148 (ill.)
   Spanish merchant ships
      protection,
      A: 64, 67, 106
Washington, George
   A: 138–39
   PS: 98
Watch list of intellectual
   property piracy. *See* Country
   Watch List
Water pollution
   PS: 159, 182
Watts, Elias
   PS: 51
Welsh pirates
   PS: 74–75, 83–85, 89, 92
West Africa
   B: 24, 98–99, 107, 110, 201,
      206–7

pirate attacks, **PS:** 26, 80
slave trade, **PS:** 26, 73
Weymouth (ship)
   B: 206
"When Wendy Grew Up: An
   Afterthought" (additional
   scene; *Peter Pan*)
   PS: 146, 153
Whipping. *See* Flogging
Whitehaven, England
   B: 126–28
Whitehouse, Sheldon
   PS: 206, 207
Whydah, Benin
   B: 206, 208
Whydah (ship)
   A: 107–8, 117
   B: 21, 24, 25, 25 (ill.), 26–27
Wildlife observations
   B: 66–67
William (ship)
   A: 133
Williams, Palgrave
   PS: 84
Windows software,
   piracy
   PS: 203–4
Windsor, Lord (governor of
   Jamaica)
   B: 186, 187–88
Wokou
   A: 158, 161–62
Wollstonecraft, Mary
   PS: 119
Women
   disguised as men, **B:** 45, 47,
      48–50
   role in pirate society, **B:** 56,
      144–45, 194
   role in society, **B:** 45, 52, 56
   See also Alvilda (Swedish
      female pirate); Bonny,
      Anne; Cheng I Sao; Female
      pirates; Female prisoners;
      Read, Mary

Women pirates. *See* Female pirates

Women prisoners
    pirate rules, **A:** 122, 132–33, 168
    rape and abuse, **A:** 92, 102, 168, 219

World Food Programme (WFP)
    A: 190, 203–4

World Intellectual Property Organization
    PS: 208

World Wars I and II
    PS: 158

Wright, Colin
    PS: 192

Writing and reading
    B: 69

Wyeth, N.C.
    A: 229
    PS: 130

Y

Yankee (ship)
    A: 151

Yellow fever
    B: 206

Yusef Reis. *See* Ward, John

Yusuf, Abdullahi
    PS: 185

Z

Zangger, Eberhard
    PS: 2

Zeus (god)
    PS: 2, 7, 8–9, 11

Zheng Chenggong. *See* Kuo Hsing Yeh

Zheng He
    A: 160–61, 160 (ill.)

Zheng Jing
    B: 146

Zheng Zhilong. *See* Ching-Chi-Ling

Zulfiquar sword
    B: 14